Copyright 2009 by the author of this book, Matt Smith. The book author retains sole copyright to his contributions to this book. All photographs taken by Matt Smith.

COVER PHOTOGRAPHS - Top (Ipswich Wanderers), Bottom (Hadleigh United).

> Published by Blackline Press
> www.blacklinepress.com
> info@blacklinepress.com
> ISBN 978-0-9563238-0-4

The Blurb-provided layout designs and graphic elements are copyright Blurb Inc., 2009. This book was created using the Blurb creative publishing service. The book author retains sole copyright to his or her contributions to this book.

blurb.com

Ram Meadow, BURY TOWN

Blackline|Press

THE REAL TRACTOR BOYS

A tour of non-league football grounds in Suffolk
by a Manchester City fan

Matt Smith

LINE UP

1	Introduction
2.	AFC Sudbury v Canvey Island
3.	Hadleigh United v Diss Town
4.	Ipswich Wanderers v Antigua & Barbuda
5.	Bury Town v Ipswich Town
6.	Long Melford v AFC Sudbury
7.	Felixstowe & Walton United v Wroxham
8.	Needham Market v Whitton United
9.	Stowmarket Town v Ipswich Wanderers
10.	Halftime
11.	Haverhill Rovers v Ely City
12.	Newmarket Town v March Town United
13.	Walsham-le-willows v Wivenhoe Town
14.	Whitton United v Lowestoft Town
15.	Woodbridge Town v AFC Sudbury
16.	Brantham Athletic v Long Melford
17.	Debenham LC v Gorleston
18.	Leiston v Ipswich Town
19.	Cornard United v Debenham LC
20.	Mildenhall Town v Histon Reserves
21.	Kirkley & Pakefield v Dereham Town
22.	Cornard United v Swaffham Town
23.	Lowestoft Town v Kirkley & Pakefield
24.	Final Score
25.	The Real Tractor Boys Awards
26.	Map Of Suffolk
27.	Post Match Comment *by Graham Smith*

INTRODUCTION

It is a long drive home to Ipswich from Manchester and it seems twice as long when my beloved Manchester City have lost. The M6 is depressing at the best of times but it is the thought of the A14 still to come that is the killer. The day had started out so well. Having left Ipswich at 8am, I had arrived at my Dad's house in Northampton just before 10am. A quick cup of tea and a bacon sandwich and we were on the road. We were heading for Eastlands and City's last home game of the season versus relegation threatened Fulham.

What has this got to do with non-league clubs in Suffolk? Well I was born in Ashton-Under-Lyne, Greater Manchester. At the age of 6 we moved to a small village in rural Norfolk called Swanton Abbott, approximately half way between Norwich and the coast and the birthplace of my Mum. I spent an idyllic few years with my two younger sisters and younger brother attending the tiniest of village schools. There were three classes and a total of 60 kids. I remember that there were only four boys and six girls in my year. If only I was interested in girls at the time!

We lived in Swanton Abbott until I was in the final year of primary school. Dad got a new job in Northampton, a town we had no connection with, and so off we moved again. I started another new school and all the boys played football at lunchtime. And they all supported a team. Throughout this football free early childhood, my Dad had shown no interest in the sport either. This being despite the fact that he had been an extremely good player. In fact, my Dad played for England at schoolboy level against Scotland. He was signed to Bury and then Bolton Wanderers as a schoolboy and was offered a professional contract, only for his father to insist on him going to university. The chance of becoming a pro had been missed but Dad had a successful semi pro career playing for Ashton United, Winsford United and Northwich Victoria .

Breaking the same ankle three times meant three things: firstly it finally ended his football career in his late 20s; secondly it put him off football for several years; and finally it meant that he now qualifies for a Blue Badge parking permit because of the dreadful physiotherapy the received at the time.

THE REAL TRACTOR BOYS

So I think my Dad was a little surprised when I asked him which football team I should support. I distinctly remember him saying "Well not Man United, that's for sure!" I recall returning to my bedroom and opening a Panini sticker album I had been given. I looked at the Manchester United page and wondered why I had been forbidden from supporting one of the only teams I had heard of. I turned one page back. It was Manchester City. "What's this all about?" I thought. Another team from Manchester, but this team are in blue, not red. Back downstairs I went. "How about Manchester City, Dad?" "Yep, that's fine" he replied. And that was that. No long-standing family tradition passed down from generation to generation. I pretty much made it up myself. At least I can still say my roots are in Manchester.

Fast forward 19 years and I was soaking up the atmosphere before City's last home game. The sun was shining and kids were playing football and basketball and scrambling up a climbing wall - all things put on by the club for the end of the season. The sponsors had provided a brand new car for someone in the ground to win that day. We entered the ground and everyone was watching Chelsea beat Man United on TVs positioned throughout the concourse. We took our seats to watch the FA Cup winning youth team complete a lap of honour. There was a certain 'aren't we great' feeling about the place. And so it continued. The game started and City were on fire. Martin Petrov and the Brazilian Elano were playing really well. The fact that this coincided with the sun shining again, was not missed.

City went in at half time 2-0 up, a result that would relegate Fulham. My Dad had put a bet on us winning 4-0 and we were worried that we had been too conservative in our prediction.

The score remained 2-0 until the 70th minute. How the game ended 20 minutes later with Fulham winning 3-2, I still do not know. It was typical Manchester City. We are really good at that sort of thing. We were the team that launched Fulham's successful run that climaxed with them staying in the Premier League.

That drive home was particularly bad. Of course I had driven home after defeats before. Usually worse games too. Losing 1-0 to teams like Middlesbrough after a Sun Jihai own goal is a regular occurrence, but this one just seemed too unfair.

It had been a funny season. The arrival of the former Thai Prime Minister as chairman, who employed the former England Manager Sven-Goran Eriksson as team manager had given us the hope of a new dawn. This had been reinforced with the arrival of a number of relatively unknown, but expensive, foreign signings. I had been to a number of games including away trips to West Ham, Fulham, Spurs, Reading and even the long trek to Newcastle, with just one win amongst them. But I love visiting new football grounds. Grounds that I have never been to. But it is so expensive.

In an ideal World I would watch every City game. If at all possible, I would get a Season Ticket. But I simply cannot afford it. So during the six-hour drive home, I started to think of other challenges I could do. I have a real interest in non-league football, probably because of Dad's history and used to watch loads of teams around Northampton, such as Kettering Town, Northampton Spencer, Cogenhoe United and Rushden Town (now Rushden & Diamonds). I had previously thought about picking a local team at the start of the FA Cup and then going to every game following the team that win. I decided against this though because I could end up having to go to Old Trafford.

And so the idea to visit every non-league club in Suffolk was born. I moved to Ipswich in 2005 with my then girlfriend, Gemma, now wife. We had met in Northampton where she was a student but she had always planned to come 'home'. I had already visited a number of non-league clubs in the area but I decided to start all over again and see how quickly I could achieve my goal.

This is my diary.

THE REAL TRACTOR BOYS

AFC SUDBURY v CANVEY ISLAND

RYMAN LEAGUE DIVISION ONE NORTH PLAY-OFF SEMI FINAL Tuesday 29 April 2008

Initially it seemed obvious to start my tour of every non-league club in Suffolk at the start of a new season however whilst flicking through the local paper, it soon became apparent that there were a couple of games at the business end of the season too good to miss.

I had been to see a few games at AFC Sudbury's King's Marsh Stadium before. I knew how to get to the ground so it seemed like a good place to start.

The club was created in 1999 after Sudbury Town and Sudbury Wanderers merged. The newly formed AFC Sudbury played in the Eastern Counties League and soon became a dominant force, going on to win 5 Championship titles before accepting an invitation to move up to the Ryman League Division One North.

The stadium has recently been developed but I feel it lacks a certain amount of character structurally. The approach is along a single track lane past the sewage works, which can make for a rather aromatic entrance on windy days. The turnstiles are located within what can only be described as a windowless conservatory, being constructed of UPVC plastic. Behind each goal there is covered terracing capable of accommodating three deep. Level with the centre line of one side of the pitch is the main stand, built in 1993, which can seat approximately 200 people. On one side of the main stand is a toilet block, with a snack bar on the other. Directly opposite the main stand is 'The Shed', a tiered and covered terrace, built in 2000, which can house another 300 fans.

Although crowds rarely average above the 350 mark, the King's Marsh Stadium has quite an atmosphere. There is a strong, singing following, complete with drums. They sing Sudbury songs and really make you feel that you are watching football at a higher level.

The game I decided to watch was the Ryman League Division One North Play-Off Semi Final (breathe in!). This is level 4 of non-league football. Promotion from this division would be to the Ryman Premier League. Beyond that is the Blue Square South; Blue Square Premier; and then onto professional league football in the Football League Division Two.

AFC Sudbury made the play-offs last season but lost 4-2 away to Enfield. Would it be second time lucky for Suffolk's highest placed non-league club and the dizzy heights of the Ryman Premier, rubbing shoulders with the likes of Billericay Town and Heybridge Swifts? Unlike the professional play-offs, this game was a one-off on the night with the winner going straight to the final to face the winners of Redbridge (managed by former Wimbledon and Bolton striker Dean Holdsworth) and Ware. As

THE REAL TRACTOR BOYS

Sudbury finished in 2nd spot, they had home advantage against 5th place Canvey Island.

Living in Ipswich, the drive to Sudbury takes about 40 minutes. The skies looked grey and as I parked my car in Brundon Lane, the first few spots of rain were beginning to fall. As I put my coat on I could hear a group of beer laden, Canvey fans a street away chanting "We are the Canvey boys, Wuh uh".

I paid my £7 admission fee, got a programme and went and stood behind the far goal. I'm not a fan of sitting to watch football and, given a choice, I would always rather stand. The atmosphere inside the ground was hotting up nicely with the singing Sudbury fans occupying one half of The Shed and the 'Canvey Boys' the other. I had read on the Canvey Island website earlier that day, that a couple of coaches were leaving Essex at 5pm and sure enough, everywhere I looked, seemed to be Canvey fans. I then remembered that both teams play in yellow so ascertaining who was supporting who would not be so easy.

I knew that Canvey Island had been higher in the football pyramid in years gone by. I remember watching them play on television in the FA Cup, knocking out Northampton Town, when I lived in Northampton. I also remember seeing Julian Dicks play for the Essex club. Whether it is true or not, the story that Dicks used to have a Big Mac and a fag at half time when playing for West Ham, still makes me smile. Checking out the pen pictures of the visitors, I was excited to see that Canvey Island had three international players in their squad albeit for Dominica and Guyana. Still, sounds good.

As the players ran out onto the pitch the weather took a turn for the worse and the rain began to fall heavily. The contest started lively and Canvey took a well deserved lead in the 21st minute, with striker Ian Luck doing well to intercept a poor Sudbury back pass. It was when the goal went in that I realised I was standing with a group of Canvey fans and the score line appeared to give them vocal confidence. One particular chap who bore a remarkable resemblance to the Harry Enfield character, Wayne Slobb, was especially vocal in his hatred of the officials and love of Canvey. One of his beloved players was adjudged to be offside by the linesman (I refuse to use the term 'assistant referee') and Wayne bellowed "You're a fucking cheat linesman!" (He obviously agreed with my feelings regarding the 'assistant referee' label). "That was never offside. You're a cheating bastard!" You could actually see the spit leaving his mouth, despite the rain. Perhaps he wasn't offside I thought. His mate, a geeky looking guy with a Canvey Island rucksack on, turned to Wayne after the passionate, but offensive, outburst and questioned "Was he offside then?" To which Wayne calmly responded "Yeah I think so."

This verbal abuse of officials and players never ceases to amaze me. In a crowd of 30,000 fans singing and chanting, the booing of the referee seems natural and almost harmless. But at this level it is one guy shouting at another guy (in this case the linesman) standing just metres in front of him and it seems so much more personal. I always admire the composure of the person being abused. It certainly puts me off ever even considering being an official. In years of watching non-league football, I have only ever seen one person react. It was a game between Needham Market and Ipswich Wanderers (more on those teams later). I seem to remember that it was a cup game and Needham were winning comprehensively. A supporter shouted something at the Wanderer's striker, Sam Banya. I have a horrible feeling the comments were of a racial nature. Banya reacted badly (and I don't blame him) and approached the spectator concerned, requesting him to repeat the comments to his face. The referee immediately intervened and sent Banya off. The offending fan continued to watch the game. Where is the justice in that? Why players and officials are seen as fair game is beyond me. Some fans seem to think that the right to abuse is part of the admission fee.

Another decision by the referee in favour of Sudbury encouraged a female Canvey fan to shout out "You're a prick referee!" In response her boyfriend declared rather embarrassingly, "You can't say that sweetheart". Wow, I thought. Music to my ears! He continued "You have to say you're a *fucking* prick referee". Oh, I thought. Silly me!

Sudbury managed to get a goal back, so at half time, it was 1-1. A competitive and exciting game. Time for a cup of tea and a trip to the toilet, but this meant braving the elements away from the protection of the covered terrace. The queue, considering the half time whistle had just been blown, was not too bad but I was very quickly soaking wet. A young lad, probably about 7 years old, joined the queue. He had closely cropped hair and was wearing a Canvey Island tracksuit and had a £5 note between his teeth. A nearby adult, who obviously knew him, asked if he was going to buy a burger and chips or just chips. He looked a little pensive and then replied "Do I have to have anything else with just chips?" which caused a ripple of laughter in the queue.

It is funny how tasty the simple things in life can be. Sometimes beans on toast can seem like a gourmet meal if you are really hungry. And on this rain soaked April evening, the cup of tea and Kit Kat I consumed at half time really hit the spot.

As the second half kicked off, Sudbury looked like they had been equally refreshed during the interval and created two great chances, only to squander them. Sudbury were punished for their misses as only a few minutes later Canvey regained the lead with a sweet header from former Peterborough United player Leon Gordon. There continued to be a number of chances as the rain fell, meaning that the ball was getting stuck in the mud and the surface water was causing problems for both defences. In the 75th minute, the goal of the game was scored as Sudbury top scorer, Jaime Rowe, fired a 25 yard screamer past Canvey's veteran goalkeeper Mel Cappleton. This took the game to extra time.

I texted Gemma to tell her that I would be home later than expected as the game had gone to extra time. "You are dedicated....and mad" came her response. I replied saying that I can't fall at the first hurdle if I am going to do this challenge!

Chances were few and far between as the conditions made playing decent football almost impossible. The players were visibly tired and understandably so. I was beginning to think about which end the penalty kicks would be taken and to take a gamble on a good spot, when Leon Gordon rose high to head a ball from a free kick past the Sudbury keeper in the 113th minute. The final whistle was blown just a few minutes later.

The Sudbury players fell to their knees, while the Canvey Island squad sprinted with renewed vigour to their travelling fans to celebrate. It was hard on Sudbury but I felt they had missed their chances earlier in the second half. In *NonLeague Today* the

Sudbury manager Mark Morsley said "I'm bitterly disappointed but we so nearly did it. My faith in this squad has been renewed and we'll just have to use this pain to drive us to greater things."

I ran back to my car, the muddy puddles having soaked my feet and the bottom of my jeans. I switched on BBC Radio Five to hear that Manchester United had beaten Barcelona one nil to make the Champions League final in Moscow. I was cold, wet and late, but not one part of me regretted my decision to watch Sudbury instead of staying on the sofa to watch United on TV. My £7 was well worth the entertainment and my challenge to visit every club in Suffolk had begun.

AFC SUDBURY 2 – 3 CANVEY ISLAND (aet) *Attendance 437 @ King's Marsh Stadium*

EXTRA TIME - But how did Canvey Island get on? Despite my fear that they would have been so physically drained after beating AFC Sudbury, they actually went on to beat Redbridge on penalties (after a 1-1 draw) to take their place in the Ryman Premier Division. The AFC Sudbury manager, Mark Morsley resigned a couple of weeks later.

CLUB INFO

ADDRESS - AFC Sudbury, King's Marsh Stadium, Brundon Lane, SUDBURY, Suffolk CO10 1XR
WEBSITE - www.afcsudbury.com
ADMISSION - £7.00 + £1.50 programme
MILES TO & FROM CLUB – 45.4 miles

THE REAL TRACTOR BOYS

THE BRETT SIDER

Official Programme
Club Website : www.hadleigh-utd.co.uk

Welcome to the Millfield

Main Club Sponsor
Hadleigh Tyre Group

Hadleigh United
Versus
Diss Town
Saturday 3rd May 2008
Kick Off 3pm
Ridgeons League Division One

HADLEIGH UNITED v DISS TOWN

RIDGEONS EASTERN COUNTIES LEAGUE DIVISION ONE
Saturday 3 May 2008

It was actually when I was on the AFC Sudbury website when I spotted this fixture. A local football news link stated that Diss Town had employed a new manager, as the club looked to gain promotion at fellow high-fliers, Hadleigh United. I could not believe my eyes when I read that the Norfolk club's new boss was former Manchester City player Robert Taylor.

City signed Taylor for £1.5million from Gillingham, during the summer of 1999. Joe Royle, and the City fans, had witnessed Taylor's work first hand as he had scored for the Kent club to put them 2-0 up against City in the play-off final at Wembley. Taylor had struck in the 86th minute and the City fans had started to leave, resigning themselves to another season in the third tier of English football.

I was watching the game in a pub in Norfolk, whilst on a short break with friends. I had taken a selection of Manchester City shirts for each pal to wear and we had emptied the pub upon arrival. I do not recall ever buying a drink. Every time I looked to my side a new pint had arrived and my girlfriend at the time kept a conveyor belt of roll-ups fully stocked. As Taylor's late strike settled in the net, I remember storming out of the pub into the garden and kicking a plant pot in frustration. I was rather drunk by this time and very upset. I made my way back inside, just in time to see Kevin Horlock pull back a goal. And then 6 minutes of extra time were declared! When Paul Dickov scored the equaliser I went mad. I could not believe it. The 30 minutes of extra time was simply a blur and I'm not sure I remember the penalty kicks from the actual day or from watching them so many times on video since. Nicky Weaver was the hero for City as we won and went back up to Division One, now known as the Championship. I finished the game by being sick back at the caravan and then sleeping in the back of the car all the way home to Northampton. It was a fantastic day!

And so Robert Taylor joined the club that robbed him of glory at Wembley. His time at City was not great; scoring 5 goals in just 16 appearances before moving to Wolves. He did however state in a recent interview that he enjoyed his time at City and stated that George Weah (who spent an equally short time at Maine Road) was the best player he ever played with. Taylor's time with Wolves was ruined by injuries and his playing career then fell away with moves to QPR, Grimbsy, back to Gillingham on loan, and finally ending up at Scunthorpe United. Taylor decided to head home to Norfolk after his playing career ended and managed Watton United and Dereham Town, before taking the Diss Town job.

I am not sure why Diss Town had sacked their previous manager considering a win at Hadleigh gave them a chance of promotion - depending upon results elsewhere. But it was Hadleigh United who were in the driving seat. If they won the game they would be promoted and it was for this reason that they were expecting a record attendance at the idyllic Millfield Ground. The previous highest attendance of 518 was set in January 1995 for an FA Vase replay with Essex club Halstead Town.

Despite being just 20 minutes from my house, I had never been to watch Hadleigh. I had read in the local press that the club was suffering financially and that they had been unable to complete the refurbishment of the clubhouse. They had also been unable to pay their players any cash in recent seasons and were only able to reward their physical efforts with a free pint after the game...in the half built clubhouse. It was because of this that I had assumed that the ground would not be worth a visit. How wrong could I be!

Hadleigh itself is a picturesque town with a population of 7000. The Millfield ground is within walking distance of the town centre and is alongside the River Brett. In complete contrast to my wet visit to Sudbury just a few days earlier, the sun was shining and Gemma decided to come along as well. Although

The Diss away fans

The main stand at Millfields

Gemma shares an Ipswich Town season ticket with her brother, it is fair to say that she is not the biggest football fan in the World. She enjoys watching Town but mainly for the social side of seeing her family who all sit in a row at Portman Road. She also sits through televised Manchester City games in the pub but only really out obligation having made me move to Suffolk almost four years ago. So the fact that she agreed to come along to Hadleigh was a nice surprise.

Extra car parking spaces had been made available and an elderly gentleman was directing vehicles upon our arrival. We paid our £4 admission fee and went to find a spot in the sun. The pitch is surrounded by white railings and a concrete path. Behind each goal is simply grass but one end is slightly banked. Having passed through the turnstiles you find yourself immediately behind the dug outs. To the right is the club house and to the left, the refreshment kiosk. The area between the clubhouse and the pitch is quite narrow, accommodating four deep at a push, but is covered. On the other side of the pitch, opposite the dug outs and club house, is the main stand. The wooden structure can seat 250 spectators on tiered benches, but no individual seats are available. That said; it is this sort of stand that interests me and not the new, prefabricated steel structures that are appearing at non-league grounds around the country.

Founded in 1892, you get a real feeling that the club is at the heart of the community – a good old fashioned club. And on a summer's day I could not think of a better place to spend the afternoon. There was a real end-of-season party atmosphere and particular efforts appeared to have been made to involve the youth teams. When the first team came out, so did one of the youth teams and they were allowed to warm up as if they were about to play. It was a delight to see.

Hadleigh were wearing their home kit of white shirts and navy blue shorts, but the strip looked tired, as if it had been worn for a number of seasons. The club sponsors, Hadleigh Tyre Group, must be disappointed that their name was disappearing from every shirt, as many of the felt letters had worn away. Diss on the other hand looked impressive in their bright, all-orange kit with Robert Taylor strolling around in front of his dug out with purpose, in a t-shirt, shorts and trainers.

The quality of play did look a level or two below the match I had been treated to on Tuesday night and it was an own goal clanger that gave Diss Town the lead. Diss had arrived to stifle play and Hadleigh seemed to be struggling with stage fright. Within just a few minutes of the opening goal, Diss scored again to make it 2-0 and Hadleigh really looked on the ropes. We decided to grab a snack just before the half time rush. Whilst ordering a cheese burger, Hadleigh managed to pull a goal back, nicely setting up the second half.

During half time the youth teams were in a penalty competition. It ended up with one, quite tall lad of about 13 against a really young and small lad who could easily have been just 8 or 9. The eldest lad was using power that the younger lad did not have. He was using skill and was knocking in some fantastic penalties that I would have been proud of. These two just kept going. When one scored, so did the other. When one missed, so did the other. Eventually, the public announcer had to declare "Listen lads, we'll have to continue this after the match. I know it's important to

THE REAL TRACTOR BOYS

you but this match is pretty important too."

But the second half failed to live up to the billing. No further goals were scored despite a few good chances and the game finished 2-1 to Diss Town.

Results elsewhere meant that neither team had achieved their goal of promotion to the Ridgeons Eastern Counties League Premier Division. That honour fell to Whitton United, who had beaten Godmanchester Rovers 5-0. I was quite pleased as Whitton are the nearest club to my house so I was looking forward to seeing them later.

In the local press the Hadleigh manager, Steve Jay said "We didn't really perform. We haven't really played well for a few weeks. But we kept getting results and other results went for us. You have to dust yourself down and get on with it. We'll have to really go for promotion next season."

HADLEIGH UNITED 1 – 2 DISS TOWN *Attendance 324 @ The Millfield*

EXTRA TIME – A week later Hadleigh United played in the Suffolk Senior Cup Final at Portman Road against lower league opposition, Grundisburgh, in front of an attendance of over 1000. Unfortunately, despite going into halftime with a 2-1 lead, they lost the game 3-2. A disappointing end to the season.

CLUB INFO

ADDRESS – Hadleigh United FC, The Millfield, Tinkers Lane, Hadleigh, IPSWICH Suffolk IP7 5NG
WEBSITE – www.hadleigh-utd.co.uk
ADMISSION - £4.00 + £1.00 programme
MILES TO & FROM CLUB – 21.4 miles

IPSWICH WANDERERS v ANTIGUA & BARBUDA

POST SEASON INTERNATIONAL FRIENDLY Saturday 31 May 2008

So the football season had come to a close. All of the play-offs, cup finals and last league games had been played and I was starting to look forward to Euro 2008, albeit minus England. And then, whilst surfing the net looking for pre-season friendly fixtures, the words 'Ipswich Wanderers v Antigua & Barbuda' stood out like a beacon. What was this all about?

I dug deeper and it turned out that former Ipswich Town player,

Norwich City & Northern Ireland manager Bryan Hamilton had been employed by the Antigua & Barbuda FA as technical director. He was then joined by former Manchester City and Ipswich Town Assistant Manager Willie Donachie as coach. Their task was to prepare Antigua & Barbuda for the biggest game in their history - a World Cup 2010 Qualifier against fellow Caribbean island Cuba. Hamilton and Donachie used their Ipswich Town connections to set up a two week training camp for the players in the UK at the Ipswich Town Training Centre. A local coach company was recruited to bus the squad around, the owner of which is the chairman of Eastern Counties League side Ipswich Wanderers FC. With tongue in cheek, he apparently asked if Antigua fancied a game against his team as a warm up. And that was that – Ipswich Wanderers would be playing an international side for the first time in their history.

OK, so Antigua & Barbuda are not a major force in World football. In fact they are ranked 127th in the World by the governing body FIFA and their team only features three full time professionals. The population of Antigua & Barbuda is 82,000 – two thirds of the population of Ipswich! But they are an international team nonetheless. The club decided to make a day of it with a steel band, lots of press coverage, invited a few famous faces and charged £7.00 to get in.

The venue for this summer festival of football was the Wanderers home ground in the wonderfully named Humber Doucy Lane (sounds brilliant in a Suffolk accent). The official name of the actual ground is the SEH Sports Ground (SEH is a local glass company) but this name is rarely used. Now I must admit a certain amount of bias at this point. I have a soft spot for Ipswich Wanderers and have watched them quite a few times. Their ground is pretty knackered, with rotting wood, broken windows, lots of corrugated iron and a bumpy pitch...and I love it. It oozes character and just smells of football. No sign of pre-fabricated stands here.

Upon entering though the turnstile, you enter a small concreted courtyard area. The bar, 'The Wander-Inn', is to the right, the club shop and snack bar to the left and the main terrace beyond that. Further along after the main terrace is the small stand which can seat 50 spectators. Back to the courtyard and beyond the bar is the covered terrace behind the goal. Whilst it can only

THE REAL TRACTOR BOYS

Ipswich Wanderers line up to face Antigua & Barbuda

accommodate a couple of rows of people deep, it is locally known as the 'Kesgrave End' and is home for small group of extremely vocal supporters who are rarely seen without a pint in hand.

Wanderers are a relatively young football club being founded in 1980 as an Under-14s boy's team. It was in 1987 that they became founding members of the Eastern Counties League Division One and made their home at Humber Doucy Lane.

The club has yo-yoed between Division One and the Premier League, but the highlight of their short history, started with the arrival of former Ipswich Town and Tottenham player Jason Dozzell as player-manager in 2003. A local boy, born and bred in Ipswich, Dozzell played 332 games for Town before moving to Spurs in a £1.9million deal. He spent four years with the north London club, then going on to play for Colchester United and Northampton Town. Dozzell stayed in charge at Wanderers for a couple of years, gaining promotion to the Premier League, before leaving to manage Suffolk rivals Leiston FC.

Last season was a really bad one for Wanderers. During the summer of 2007, their manager John Clarkson resigned, taking his money with him. This meant that a lot of the players left too. Two managers later, and after some embarrassingly heavy defeats, Wanderers were related back to Division One. The chance to play a Caribbean nation was therefore a great way to lift everyone's spirits. I arrived at the ground at 1.30, for an earlier than usual 2pm kick off, on a gloriously sunny late May afternoon. The club was hoping for a bumper crowd with lots of coverage in the local press and even a special feature on BBC Radio Suffolk's black current affairs programme 'Ebony Eye'.

There were a number of cars in the car park, however a gleaming black Range Rover with a private number plate stood out. I immediately recognised that it was the former Ipswich Town defender Titus Bramble's motor. Ironically, I had just been reading about Bramble in 442 Magazine as he qualifies through his grandparents to play for another Caribbean nation, Montserrat. Famously ranked the worst international team in the World, Montserrat are apparently trying to persuade the Wigan Athletic defender to play for them, in the hope that he could bring some Premier League experience to their obviously frail back four.

It was such a nice day that I decided to have a beer and that is when I came face to face with Titus. I was taken aback by his size. He is a big man and it makes you realise just how deceiving the television can be. He was joined by his older brother, Tes, who is also a footballer having played for Southend United and Stockport County. Tes had just been released by Stevenage Borough, so perhaps Wanderers were trying to sign him up! Unlike his brother, Tes is a striker and has pledged his allegiance to Montserrat, having already gained one international cap.

Obviously Willie Donachie and Bryan Hamilton were there with their squad of international footballers, however that was not the end of the famous faces. Next on the radar was Wanderer's former manager and previously mentioned Jason Dozzell and he was with Ipswich Town legend Kevin Beattie. Regarded as one of the greatest Ipswich Town players ever, Beattie was a defender dubbed 'the new Bobby Moore' and played for the club during the 1970s. His manager, Bobby Robson, once declared that Beattie could have easily become the most capped player in the history of English football. Persistent injuries limited him to 9 games for England and an early retirement at the age of 28. Sporting some designer glasses and a rather snazzy ear stud, I overheard Beattie decline the offer of some chips from a mate, declaring that he had just had two poached eggs on four rounds of toast at a local café and was absolutely stuffed. He decided to have a fag instead.

THE REAL TRACTOR BOYS

The winner of the inaugural PFA Young Player of the Year in 1974 is just a normal bloke!

And so to the game. It was a rather bizarre affair. I could not help but wonder what the visiting players made of the whole thing. To start with I had never seen a bigger, stronger, fitter looking team line up at Humber Doucy Lane – I am referring to the Antiguans! They looked immense. Before kick off was an international style line up, team photos and the exchange of pennants. I even thought they were going to play the national anthems over the public address system.

The game was pretty good for a friendly. To be honest, Wanderers looked like a team that had just played a whole season and been relegated and Antigua looked like a group of strong athletes who had never played football before, certainly not together. That said it made for an interesting contest. Antigua grew in confidence and cohesion taking the lead just before half time. Unfortunately I was waiting for a burger at the snack bar so did not really get a good view of the goal. It was scored in the 41st minute by Troy Simon who met a cross by Gayson Gregory (a

The Antigua & Barbuda flag draped in front of the main stand.

full time professional player in Trinidad).

Both of the teams stayed out on the pitch at half time, simply basking in the sun. On the hour, Antigua doubled their lead with a great move, culminating in a goal for Peter Byers. During the 2nd half, the Antiguan management team used all of their 20-strong squad in Sven-Goran Eriksson style, however they went one step further with some of their players coming on for Wanderers.

After the game, Bryan Hamilton said that it had been a great exercise for his squad. He would obviously now turn his attentions to the game against Cuba and his quest to reach South Africa in 2010. I could not help but feel that a part of Ipswich will be looking out for their results and wishing them all the best.

IPSWICH WANDERERS 0 – 2 ANTIGUA & BARBUDA
Attendance 205 @ Humber Doucy Lane

EXTRA TIME – Despite the efforts of Bryan Hamilton, Willie Donachie and their trip to Suffolk, Antigua & Barbuda were beaten 4-3 at home against Cuba and then 4-0 away in Havana. Cuba progressed to the group stage, drawn together with Guatemala, Trinidad & Tobago and the USA. The road to the World Cup in South Africa in 2010 was over.

CLUB INFO

ADDRESS – SEH Sports Ground, Humber Doucy Lane, IPSWICH, Suffolk IP4 3N
WEBSITE - www.ipswichwanderersfc.co.uk
ADMISSION - £7.00 + £1.00 programme
MILES TO & FROM CLUB – 8.2 mile

THE REAL TRACTOR BOYS

Official Matchday Programme
Sponsored by Premier Printers Ltd

Bury Town
vs
Ipswich Town

Wednesday 9th July 2008
Pre-Season Friendly
Welcome to Ram Meadow

BURY TOWN v IPSWICH TOWN

PRE SEASON FRIENDLY Wednesday 9th July 2008

So the Tractor Boys visit my 'real' Tractor Boys. A game not to be missed! Ipswich Town are actually very supportive of the local non-league teams, and often play a number of them in pre season friendly fixtures. They have also recently re-entered a team in the Suffolk Premier Cup and a home tie against Town guarantees a crowd and a big pay day.

Bury Town (from Bury St Edmunds and not to be confused with Bury in Greater Manchester!) are recognised as one of the oldest

THE REAL TRACTOR BOYS

non-league clubs in the country, being founded in 1872. The club has been relatively successful during their history, playing in a number of leagues and recently reached the semi final of the FA Vase, only to get knocked out by Hillingdon Borough in front of a crowd of 1,773.

Bury Town's ground is called Ram Meadow and is one of my favourites in Suffolk. It is located just a short walk from the picturesque centre of Bury St Edmunds, with a large pay & display car park right outside (free to park after 6pm) and in view of the grand St Edmundsbury Cathedral. The town's folk turn out and support Bury for the big games, however I have always felt that average attendances of around 200 are poor for a town of over 35,000 people.

After going through the turnstile you enter a small concreted area at the corner of the pitch. Preceding straight ahead, the club house, bar and club shop are alongside the pitch. The foreground between the building and the pitch is covered. Having walked past the club house there is a burger van and then level with the centre line of the pitch is the main stand. This rather grand, wooden structure only seats about 100 despite its size and most of the seats appear to be reserved for club officials and guests. Behind each goal are covered, good sized terraces named the Car Park End and the River End. I think these are my favourite terraces of all the grounds in Suffolk. Opposite the main stand is another covered seating area. Called the G Taylor Construction Stand, it is fitted with long wooden benches rather than individual seats. This is a great stand offering a good view of the pitch.

Ipswich Town sent a pretty good squad for this fixture, albeit effectively a reserve team. The club was due to head off to Northern Ireland for a summer tour and had scheduled high profile friendlies against Premier League teams; West Ham United and West Bromwich Albion. This game was therefore seen as a run out for some of the fringe players with Shane Supple, Matt Richards, Gary Roberts, Dean Bowditch, Jaime Peters and Billy Clarke all starting. The manager Jim Magilton was absent, so newly employed Reserve Team Development Coach, Chris Kiwomya, took charge.

Kiwomya needs no introduction to Ipswich Town fans, having

made 259 appearances for the Portman Road club. He scored 64 goals before moving to Arsenal for £1.25million in 1995. Before rejoining Ipswich he had been working for the academy at Arsenal but is still a big figure in Ipswich. In fact a friend of mine had recently met him in a queue outside an Ipswich night club. He had paid for her and her friends to get into the club even though she had no idea of who he was, this despite the rest of the queue chanting his name!

The headline news for me however was someone who would be playing for Bury Town - the former Northern Ireland international Kevin Horlock. Horlock played for Ipswich Town between 2004 and 2006 making 58 appearances but it his six year spell with Manchester City that obviously meant more to me. He scored 39 goals for City including a vital strike in the previously mentioned 1999 play off final. How odd that in the space of a couple of months I had seen two of the goal scorers from that great game now involved in East Anglian non-league football. I was wondering when and where Paul Dickov and Carl Asaba would pop up, and then I would have the full set!

After leaving Ipswich, Horlock had spells at Doncaster Rovers, Scunthorpe United and Mansfield Town and now at the age of 35, had retired from the professional game and moved back to Suffolk, apparently to be closer to his best mate, Jaime Scowcroft (the Crystal Palace striker) who lives near Eye. Horlock did not want to stop playing though and had been training with Bury Town and would play against his former employers, but had not signed a permanent deal with the club.

Kevin Horlock is not the only former professional with Bury. Another former Ipswich player, Gavin Johnson, signed for the club in 2007. He made 131 appearances for Town between 1989 and 1995 before going on to play for Luton Town, Wigan Athletic, Dunfirmline, Colchester United, Boston United, Northampton Town and Oxford United. In goal is the well travelled veteran keeper, Dean Greygoose. Capped five times at England Under-17 level, Greygoose has an even more impressive list of former clubs including Cambridge United, Lincoln City, Leyton Orient, Crystal Palace, Crewe Alexandra, Northwich Victoria, Chester City, Stevenage Borough, Kings Lynn, AFC Sudbury and Soham Town Rangers. After 25 years of professional and semi- professional football he now runs his own coaching school as well as playing

THE REAL TRACTOR BOYS

for Bury.

And Dean's wife is also a popular character at the club. In the clubhouse, enjoying a pint before the game, I was told that Mrs Greygoose often cooks a cake for each game, for the consumption of the fans!

I went to watch the game with my Father-In-Law, an Ipswich Town season ticket holder. We had arrived at the ground in good time and had over an hour to kill before kick off, hence our presence in the bar. It was here that my Father-In-Law bumped into an old school mate whose son is a Bury Town player. He watched most of the games home and away the previous season, supporting his son and the team. He had visited the recently built and award-winning home of Dartford where Bury had won 2-1 in front of 824 fans (an excellent result considering Dartford won promotion as champions) and then a couple of weeks later he had witnessed a 2-2 draw away at Tilbury, in front of 49 spectators. The contrasts of non league football!

But that was all in the Ryman League Northern Division, a league with clubs from Suffolk, Essex and Greater London. Due to the complexities of the non-league pyramid, Bury were preparing for the new season in a new league having been moved by the FA to the British Gas Southern League, along with AFC Sudbury. This move causes considerable problems for our Suffolk clubs because the league spans the midlands, meaning longer journeys as far as Malvern Town, on the English/Welsh border. The move does not mean any more income and the Bury Town Board reckon their transport costs will increase from £9,000 a season to £12,000. Likewise, the fans have further to go and the chap I was talking to could not see himself going to every away game.

Despite the thought of pre-season friendly evening fixtures in July conjuring images of long summer nights, cool pints of beer and being bitten by insects, it had been raining all day. In fact I was surprised the game went ahead, until I realised the admission fee was £9.00. With the crowd expected to be over 1000 there was no way Bury would let this one go, especially as it would have just been cancelled and not postponed.

The club was worried that the rain would put off the fans, but a healthy crowd of 945 turned up, with a large number of Ipswich fans eager to get their first fix of football after the summer break. Ipswich starter the brighter team and the difference in class showed. The professional team took the lead half way through the first half with Dean Bowditch scoring. I now have a confession to make! Ipswich scored two more goals in quick concession just before the break. Unfortunately I missed both of them, as firstly I was walking to get a cup of tea and secondly I was queuing for a cup of tea. I was informed by the PA that Jaime Peters scored the second and Ed Upson the third.

The usual pre-season substitutions dominated the second half and with it the competitiveness disappeared. No further goals were scored and Bury managed to keep the score respectful. Kevin Horlock left the field after 70 minutes and had been fairly quiet in the game. I was disappointed that he did not get any sort of applause of any note from either set of fans. I applauded him off; thankful for *that* goal he scored for City over 8 years ago.

BURY TOWN 0 – 3 IPSWICH TOWN *Attendance 945 @ Ram Meadow*

EXTRA TIME – Kevin Horlock decided not to commit his future to Bury Town despite playing a number of pre-season friendlies. He did decide to play local non-league football though and it would not be long until I was watching him again.

CLUB INFO

ADDRESS – Bury Town FC, Ram Meadow, Cotton Lane, BURY ST EDMUNDS Suffolk IP33 1XP
WEBSITE – www.burytownfc.co.uk
ADMISSION - £9.00 + £1.00 programme
MILES TO & FROM CLUB – 51.2 miles

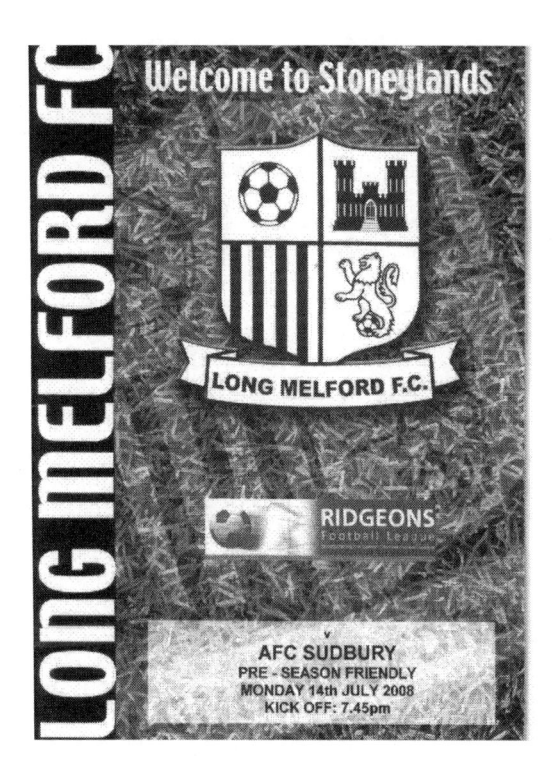

LONG MELFORD v AFC SUDBURY

PRE-SEASON FRIENDLY Monday 14th July 2008

All of the grounds I had visited up to this point are in towns of varying sizes. Long Melford is a large village of just over 3500 people, just a couple of miles to the north of Sudbury. It is an extremely picturesque village that can trace its history back to 100BC. The village is basically a 3 mile street with a few side lanes leading off. The name derives from this; *long* street and the mill ford (*melford*) that crosses the Chad Brook, a tributary of the River Stour. There are a number of beautiful houses and halls, and the village itself is a popular tourist destination.

THE REAL TRACTOR BOYS

I had originally penciled in my diary a pre-season friendly fixture between Long Melford and FC Adeje, a professional team from Tenerife, who had planned to tour the eastern counties, until their sponsor pulled out. I had been looking forward to the match and was disappointed that it was cancelled but decided to look at their other pre-season games. The visit of AFC Sudbury stood out as it is a local derby and AFC Sudbury's first game since the play-off defeat at the start of this diary.

I was rather tired during the day leading up to the rather odd Monday night fixture, and did not really fancy the 40 minute drive to watch the game but I reckoned this would be the best attended game at Melford's Stoneylands Stadium this season, so it would be silly not to go.

Despite Long Melford simply being one long street, I really struggled to find the road leading to the ground. After stopping to look at the map for the third time I eventually realised that the narrow entrance to the side of the Co-Op was not someone's driveway but was the road I was looking for. After parking the car I walked up to the ground. Turning the corner I was faced with the usual metal gates, pot holed car park and collection of wooden buildings with flood lights towering above. No turnstile at the Stoneylands Stadium. Instead two little old ladies (simply referred to as a collective 'Mrs. Mills' in the match-day programme) squeezed into the smallest shed I have ever seen. They reminded me, in a good way, of the two old ladies who run the charity shop in the sit-com, 'The League of Gentlemen'. I paid the very reasonable admission of £3.00 and picked up one of the last programmes for an extra quid.

Something the club should certainly be proud of is their programme and their website. Both look very professional and could easily be from a club playing several steps higher in the football pyramid. The programme featured a decent amount of up to date information including an interview with their latest close-season signing, and a summer diary of events at the club.

Unfortunately, the Stoneylands Stadium is not as impressive. The non-league favourites of conifer trees and corrugated iron are very much the order of the day. The entrance is at the corner of the pitch. Straight ahead, behind the goal is an open grassed area leading to the cricket club. Turn left and there is a small club house and snack bar. Next to the club house is a very odd looking covered area for standing supporters but it is set too far back from the pitch. Next is the main stand. I guess it seats approximately 100 people and is one of the prefabricated stands that are popping up at small non-league grounds across the country. I understand why clubs purchase these structures. They are relatively cheap and easy to erect. But they lack character and do nothing to differentiate one ground from another.

Behind the far end is an area of covered terrace directly behind the goal, built from corrugated iron and painted in the club colours of black and white. The opposite side of the pitch is uncovered and backed by the conifer trees. Unfortunately there is hardly any room to squeeze in between the trees and the pitch perimeter fencing.

That said, there was a lovely, friendly atmosphere and I thoroughly enjoyed my visit. It is a shame though that such a picturesque, historic village houses this sad little ground. The history books show a football team representing Long Melford as early as 1868 and they were extremely successful. One of the club's most incredible claims to fame is that between 1883 and 1888 one of their players, William Melville Cobbold actually played centre forward for the full England team!

In 1888, after another successful season, the club requested to play Ipswich Town. Town apparently declined the offer, stating that it would be 'injurious' for a club of Ipswich Town's stature to play little village teams. However, Long Melford got their wish, as in the same season they were drawn against Ipswich Town in a local cup competition and beat their illustrious county cousins 2-1. A local newspaper printed the headline 'What about the little village now!' and the club have been known as the 'The Villagers' ever since.

The club won promotion to the Ridgeons Eastern Counties League in 2002. Since moving up they have had 6 managers, including the former Cambridge United striker, John Taylor (now manager at Newmarket Town).

It is all change at AFC Sudbury, since my visit to their final game of last season. A new management team and a large number of new players. The chatter amongst the replica strip clad AFC fans was that they did not recognise nine of their own players! AFC and Long Melford are two divisions apart and this was evident just in their respective appearance. AFC wore their new, crisp yellow and blue strip, complete with club badge and sponsor. Long Melford ran out in their black and white (or more accurately grey and grey) strip that I assume had been worn for a number of seasons.

It was therefore not surprising that AFC looked the better team from the off, although they did look like they were a bunch of good footballers who had not played together before...which was true. To start with, Melford were happy to hit long balls to the rather odd strike force duo, one of whom looked remarkably similar to Meatloaf and the other, the comedian Tony Hawks. But Melford stuck at it and their determination not to let their superior neighbours run the show was great to watch. The home team held out and the teams went in at half time at 0-0.

It was at this point that I realised that in every game I had been to since the start of this journey, the home team had lost. Was I an unlucky omen? I therefore crossed my fingers for Melford in the hope that the awful run could come to an end.

The second half started brightly and AFC hit the post but the substitutions then took the sting out of the game. That was until the 85th minute when AFC took the lead, much to my annoyance, with ex-Melford player Danny Stokes scoring the goal. Delight followed soon after though, as Melford's Carl Daw equalised just a minute or so later. A 1-1 draw, and a positive result for both teams in preparation for the season to come.

LONG MELFORD 1 – 1 AFC SUDBURY *Attendance 255 @ Stoneylands Stadium*

CLUB INFO

ADDRESS – Long Melford FC, Stoneylands Stadium, New Road, Long Melford, SUDBURY, Suffolk CO10 9JY
WEBSITE – www.stoneylands.co.uk
ADMISSION - £3.00 + £1.00 programme
MILES TO & FROM CLUB – 48.8 miles

THE REAL TRACTOR BOYS

FELIXSTOWE & WALTON UNITED v WROXHAM

RIDGEONS EASTERN COUNTIES LEAGUE PREMIER DIVISION Saturday 9th August 2008

After a couple of high profile pre-season friendly fixtures, it was time to get down to business. I was determined to watch a game on the opening day of the season, but had to be back at home in time to watch Manchester City play AC Milan on Channel 5 at 5.15pm. There were limited, immediately, local options so I decided on a trip to the seaside town of Felixstowe.

With concerns that the annual Felixstowe Carnival might affect car parking, I got to 'The Town Ground' in good time. Unfortunately the weather was more akin to October and we quickly regretted not wearing more suitable clothing, as driving rain and wind howled around the ground.

Felixstowe & Walton United were formed in 2000 after Walton United merged with Felixstowe Port & Town FC. The clubs had temporarily joined forces after the 2nd World War, only to go their separate ways in 1946. With a population of around 30,000, Felixstowe is most famous for its container port, the largest in the United Kingdom. It is estimated that 35% of all containers coming to the UK do so through Felixstowe. The port is an amazing sight and operates 24 hours a day. Ship spotters regularly watch the biggest ships in the World arrive from various destinations.

The football ground shares the same site as the town's cricket club. After passing through the car park there are two club houses overlooking the cricket pitch; one for the cricket club and one for the football club. Spectators and players then have to walk along a paved path alongside the cricket pitch to reach the football pitch.

I assume that football has been played at the ground for many years however as a non-league football stadium it has a little character. Admission is paid at a little shed in the corner of the ground. A metal barrier and concrete path surrounds the pitch with sporadic advertising boards. The only structures in place are along the left hand side of the pitch. On the half way line is the dreaded pre-fabricated 200-seat stand. A little further along is a pre-fabricated covered terrace area, also capable of holding 200 fans according to the 'Non League Club Directory'. Next to the terrace is a snack van and then a small, unused, wooden building in the corner.

Behind each goal is simply grass. The opposite side of the pitch accommodates the two small team dugouts and that is it. Surrounding the ground are well established trees and thankfully no conifers. Unfortunately due to the lack of advertising boards and the large grassed areas surrounding the pitch, the players seem to spend too much of their time getting the ball back.

I was not sure how many fans would attend the game. August is a

The entrance to 'The Town Ground'.

funny time of year for football. Lots of people are excited that the season is starting again but many are on their summer holidays. The weather was horrible and Ipswich Town were playing at home and all these things affect non-league fixtures. The town of Felixstowe should be able to provide a good level of support but standing in the ground at 2.30pm and only counting 8 others, I was not optimistic. Thankfully as kick off loomed the attendance grew to 86 but considering that on the same day, further up the coast, Lowestoft Town were entertaining a crowd of 426, it is a shame the people of Felixstowe do not support their team more.

The Felixstowe programme is a great little publication. The full colour cover features a picture of the seafront and pier. Inside there are plenty of adverts but equally as much interesting stuff to read, including good information about the visiting team, other league and cup fixtures, and a really useful pen picture guide to their own players. Most programmes do not to do this and as a roaming supporter I like to read about both teams. The team sheets revealed a few names that I recognised for both teams.

I was looking forward to seeing Wroxham. The small town holds special memories for me because I lived in north Norfolk between the ages of 5 and 10, and the nearest supermarket was 'Roys of Wroxham', a strange collection of stores that dominate the village. The football club has been especially successful in recent seasons and finished third in 2007/08. Amongst their ranks is a former professional, Alex Notman. Still only 28, Notman started out as a youth player at none other than Manchester United and featured in the Scotland under-21 squad.

As with many promising youngsters, he had to move away from Old Trafford to get regular football and after loan spells at Aberdeen and Sheffield United, he moved to Norwich City in a £250,000 deal in 2000. During the East Anglian derby against Ipswich Town in 2002, he damaged his ankle ligaments, an injury that would force his retirement from the professional game the following year. In 2004, Notman signed for Norfolk non-league club King's Lynn FC, but unfortunately his persistent injuries caused him to quit the club in 2005. Two years later he made a comeback with Lincolnshire club, Boston United however shortly after his debut he moved to Wroxham in October 2007. It is always sad to hear about promising careers that have been cut short through injury, but I was looking forward to seeing a player of his undoubted quality on a rainy afternoon in Felixstowe.

I had managed to drag Gemma along to watch this game. Unfortunately she is dreadful at choosing the correct clothing to wear when going out. She often asks me how cold is it? As a bloke, I am always warmer than she is so it is irrelevant how warm or cold I think it is. Therefore it was not surprising that she was cold throughout the game. Luckily she found her own entertainment watching the toddler son of one of the Felixstowe players run up and down, in front of the terrace. Wroxham hit the woodwork twice in the first half and on each occasion I turned to her to comment on the near goal, only for her to respond that she was watching the toddler, growing more and more broody by the minute.

Wroxham took the lead after just five minutes with Paul Cook scoring with his head, a goal that the Felixstowe keeper should really have saved. Wroxham were starting to show signs of why they were, once again, being tipped as one of the title runners, but it was Felixstowe who scored next. Last seasons top scorer put away a penalty on the 20 minute mark after a foul in the box. Wroxham responded, and it seemed only a matter of time before they would retake the lead. It was the aforementioned Alex Notman who found space and scored the goal of the game from 20yards.

At half time we decided to visit the club house. As mentioned earlier, the club house is reached by walking along a paved path beside the cricket pitch. This creates a rather odd scenario where you are walking off the pitch with the players, heading for their own half-time refreshment. In fact I nearly followed them all the way in to the changing rooms.

The club house is an old wooden building which in its day must have been fairly grand. Time has taken its toll however and it now needs more than just a lick of paint. Inside is cosy, with lots of photographs and shirts adorning the walls, however there was a rather bizarre situation with an office-type partition enclosing a corner of the club house. An A4 piece of paper affixed to the partition declared that only committee members and officials were permitted beyond the partition. There, the exclusive guests were being treated to plates of sandwiches and cups of tea. It looked like a scene from several decades ago. Before I could even finish my flat, overpriced, pint of Carlsberg we heard the bell ring from the changing rooms, signaling the end of half time. We then joined the players again as we all made our way back to the pitch.

After the break, Wroxham dominated the game and two more goals from Andrew Key sealed the win. On this performance Wroxham really looked like they would be battling for honours. Felixstowe were well beaten, but showed enough in their play to suggest they would not struggle and probably end up mid table once again.

FELIXSTOWE & WALTON UNITED 1 – 4 WROXHAM
Attendance 86 @ The Town Ground

EXTRA TIME - Both teams had reverse results within just a couple of days. The following Tuesday, Felixstowe & Walton United beat Essex club Stanway Rovers 2-1 while Wroxham were beaten 3-2 in a close game away, at Lowestoft Town in front of 409 spectators.

CLUB INFO
ADDRESS – Felixstowe & Walton United FC, The Town Ground, Dellwood Avenue, FELIXSTOWE, Suffolk IP11 9HT
WEBSITE – www.felixstowe.btinternet.co.uk
ADMISSION - £5.00 + £1.00 programme
MILES TO & FROM CLUB – 26.4 mile

THE REAL TRACTOR BOYS

NEEDHAM MARKET v WHITTON UNITED

RIDGEONS EASTERN COUNTIES LEAGUE PREMIER DIVISION Tuesday 12th August 2008

Six games in to my tour of Suffolk's non league clubs, and still no home team win. I really was starting to think that I was a curse on the home team. Surely the run must come to an end with a Tuesday night visit to Bloomfields, the home of Needham Market FC.

Needham had a fantastic season last year. They missed out on

THE REAL TRACTOR BOYS

being champions and winning promotion, on the last day of the season, in a winner takes all game at eventual champions, Soham Town Rangers. They also narrowly missed out on a day at Wembley in the FA Vase, losing over to two legs to Kirkham & Wesham, in the semi. They did however manage to win the Ridgeons League Challenge Cup and the S1 Sports Suffolk Premier Cup. All in all, a very successful season. On the opening day of this campaign they beat Haverhill Rovers 4-1. In contrast, newly promoted opponents Whitton United were given a lesson in Premier League football, being beaten 8-2. Hence my optimism that the home team must win today.

Needham Market is a small town to the north of Ipswich, bypassed by the A14, with a population of just over 4,500. The town's most notable point in history was between 1663 and 1665 when the plague swept through the Needham Market. To prevent the spread of the disease the town was chained at either end. This did the job, but two thirds of the town's folk were lost. To mark this time in history one of the new housing estate roads was named Chainhouse Road, and it leads to Quinton Road and the football ground.

Gemma was born and bred in the town, so it was my first real introduction to life in Suffolk before I moved to Ipswich. Perhaps more famously though, the Eastenders actress June Brown, who plays Dot Cotton, was born in Needham Market in 1927 – hardly the east end of London!

Needham Market FC was originally founded in 1919 however it is only in recent years that the club has really progressed. It was in the 1995-96 season that the club applied to join the Eastern Counties League and moved to their current ground, Bloomfields (named after Derek Bloomfield who served the club for over 60 years in various capacities). After ten years in Division One the club won promotion to the Premier, under the management of Mark Morsley, who went on to manage AFC Sudbury. Now under the leadership of Danny Laws the club has gone from strength to strength. Last season's FA Vase run was an extremely profitable adventure and has enabled the club to make significant investment in to the ground and its facilities.

I last visited Bloomfields a couple of seasons ago to watch them play Ipswich Town Reserves in the Suffolk Premier Cup. A record attendance of 750 watched plucky Needham lose 3-0 to the reserve side put out by the professional club.

The ground is set up on a hill, overlooking the town. New, twin, turnstiles have been installed to the side of an extended clubhouse. A pathway leads you to the corner of the pitch, passing the club house entrance and brick-built snack bar. A short, but steep incline means that the pitch is almost level with the upper-floor of the club house, with steps up to the committee member's bar and steps down, to the player's changing rooms. Further along is the main stand. I am glad to say that despite this being a fairly new ground, the main stand is not the pre-fabricated rubbish seen at so many grounds across the country. It is purpose built for Bloomfields, accommodates 250 spectators, and is pretty tall but fairly functional in appearance.

Behind one goal are the club shop and a couple of small covered areas set back from the pitch perimeter. Behind the other goal is open. On the side opposite the main stand, are the dugouts and a small covered terrace area measuring half the length of the pitch. I like this terrace. Many fans take up a spot in this area, if only to listen and watch the manager, who commands his team from the sideline with great enthusiasm and colourful language.

I was especially keen to watch Needham and in particular their new player/assistant manager, Kevin Horlock. In quite a local coup, Needham had secured the services of the former Northern Ireland international from under the nose of Bury Town, despite him playing a number of games pre-season for them. The press reports stated that he had signed a lucrative deal. It did not take long for rumours to circulate the internet message boards and forums. One whisper was that Horlock had received a signing on fee of £6000 to be followed by £300 a game and £50 a goal. Quite a contract (if true) considering that the club probably only takes £750 a game in gate receipts. Also considering nearby club, Ipswich Wanderers can only currently afford to pay players £10 a match.

It was therefore concerning when I arrived in the ground, to see Horlock wearing jeans and a hoodie, standing at the sidelines just five minutes before kick off. A quick look at the team board however clearly stated that he was playing and wearing the number 4 shirt. Sure enough, when the teams ran out, there was

THE REAL TRACTOR BOYS

Kevin Horlock and I realised that I must have noticed his brother, who had come to support his sibling. The Kevin look-a-like was the joined by the rest of the family. My wife would have especially enjoyed it when a Horlock toddler had to be stopped from running on the pitch, shouting 'Daddy' when Kevin took an early corner!

Once again, the weather was extremely unseasonal. In fact, the amount of rain that had fallen earlier in the day threatened to postpone the game. Whilst the rain had stopped by the time the game kicked off, it was still pretty windy.

Surprisingly it was Whitton who started most brightly and they took a shock lead when Oliver Canfer scored with a 20 yard strike. Needham stepped up their game and following a couple of good efforts, finally won a penalty just before half time. I had been making my way around the pitch to get a cup of tea at the interval, so I was stood directly behind the goal when Kevin Horlock placed the ball on the penalty spot. He must have had his mind of the £50 extra he was about to earn because the effort was poor and easily saved by the Whitton keeper Ryan Beal, who bares a likeness to Edwin Van Der Saar from distance. In fact, Beal was having a great game and made an amazing point blank save from the resulting corner. So half time arrived and Needham were one nil down and I really started to wonder if I was a bad omen to every home team I watched.

Needham came out determined to succeed after what I assume was an unpleasant half time team talk by the gaffer. It only took the home side five minutes to equalise when Daniel Thrower scored from 25 yards. Just five minutes later Needham took the lead when the Whitton keeper Beal made his first mistake of the match, allowing James Evans to score.

Needham were now in total control and there was no doubt that they would win the match. Whitton were restricted to playing on the break and I cannot recall a second half effort on goal. The home team increased their lead when vice captain Rhys Barber scored a header from a Horlock corner. A fourth goal was scored in the 77th minute by former Felixstowe, Woodbridge and Bury Town striker, Glenn Snell.

A comprehensive victory and the second 4-1 win in four days for

Needham. The new star signing, Horlock had played well despite missing the penalty and at last the club that I had gone to visit had won a game. Needham are definitely a club on the move. The facilities are fantastic and the ground has a nice atmosphere. Everything about the club feels that little bit more professional than the others around them.

NEEDHAM MARKET 4 – 1 WHITTON UNITED
Attendance 186 @ Bloomfields

CLUB INFO

ADDRESS – Needham Market FC, Bloomfields, Quinton Road, Needham Market, IPSWICH Suffolk IP6 8DA
WEBSITE – www.needhammarketfc.co.uk
ADMISSION - £5.00 + £1.00 programme
MILES TO & FROM CLUB – 15.8 miles

STOWMARKET TOWN v IPSWICH WANDERERS

FA CUP EXTRA QUALIFYING ROUND Saturday 16th August 2008

Just a couple of miles further north from Needham Market is the larger town of Stowmarket. The town is situated slap bang in the middle of Suffolk. This obviously helps the team when they have to travel to away games. Throughout the season, Stowmarket Town FC will cover the lowest amount of miles of all the clubs in the league, traveling just 1320 miles compared to the whopping 2584 that Norfolk based, Wisbech Town will have to complete by May next year.

THE REAL TRACTOR BOYS

The FA Cup is regarded as the most famous club competition in the whole World. It is steeped in history, tradition and magic. This is the cup tournament that David gets to beat Goliath in. The cup of dreams! The competition is the oldest in the World and dates back to 1871 and a record number of 762 clubs have entered this season. The final of the 2008-2009 FA Cup will be held at the magnificent new Wembley in May 2009 and will probably feature Manchester United or Arsenal but it all starts today, in August 2008, ten months before the final. This is why the cup is so special. It involves clubs at all levels. A win at this stage of the competition means a place in the Preliminary Round and a cheque for £750 for the club.

I was quite excited when I took up my place along the side of the pitch. The team announcer introduced the two teams and declared that "The long road to Wembley starts here. You never know...you never know." The thought that the winners of this fixture could make it all the way to the 3rd Round draw and be pulled out at home to Manchester City bought a smile to my face. How fantastic that wouldbe!

Greens Meadow can be seen briefly from the A14 flyover but this was my first ever visit to the ground. After passing through the turnstile you enter the arena, level with the half way line. To the right is the main stand with benches accommodating 200 spectators. Turn left and there is a small covered terrace. Beyond the terrace is the club house and a fantastic pub-style patio area with picnic benches in the corner. The other three sides of the ground are open and grassed but there is enough at Greens Meadow to give it character and I really like it. It was therefore a shame that only 87 people turned for this local derby cup tie – not quite the estimated 480 million viewers who will tune in to watch the final on television.

The opposition were fellow Eastern Counties Division One team, Ipswich Wanderers. A quick glance at the team sheets demonstrated that the team bore little resemblance to the one I watched a couple of months earlier, playing the International Friendly match against Antigua & Barbuda. In fact the Stowmarket line-up featured a number of ex-Wanderers players. I then noticed that the Stowmarket manager was Louis Newman and he had made the move from Wanderers in the last year. An added bit of spice then!

THE REAL TRACTOR BOYS

As the game kicked off, I overheard a couple of stalwart fans discussing that the Stowmarket club captain, Chris Keys, had decided to leave the club and join Hadleigh United. The guys I were listening to seemed as devastated as Chelsea fans would be if John Terry decided to swap Stamford Bridge for the Emirates Stadium. How would this affect the team today?

The game started lively and there were some local derby crunching tackles flying around the pitch. I was immediately impressed by a lad playing for Wanderers who I had never seen before. Camillo Douglas is similar to Shaun Wright-Phillips in statue and seemed to be just as quick. He was tearing the home team's defence apart and he helped his team take an early lead. Douglas was fouled on the edge of the box and Marc Wake scored with his head, converting the resulting free kick. Wanderers' vocal and alcohol-boosted away support were positioned behind the goal and celebrated their first FA Cup strike of the season.

The home team support did not have to wait long to see their team respond. Just five minutes later they drew level from the penalty spot, with James Graham scoring, after Tom Deller had been pulled down by the Wanderers' goalkeeper. It was not a major surprise that Stowmarket had won a penalty. The Wanderers' defence were the biggest, strongest, meanest looking foursome I think I have ever seen. Whilst this brute force may be useful a lot of the time, they were not the most mobile and a foul in the box at some point, seemed inevitable.

Having drawn level, the home team went on to have the better of the play, but failed to capitalise and therefore the score remained 1-1 at half time. I decided to grab a cup of tea and flick through the match-day programme. In days gone by, football clubs at this level could never afford to print glossy colour covers for each individual match; instead every game would feature the same cover with the actual match details listed inside. Advances in printing have meant that a lot of clubs are now able to feature the match details on the cover however, the Stowmarket programme did not even feature the year the game was being played in let alone the match date, opposition or competition. Nice photographs of the ground through.

Inside, the editor states that the programme is a bumper 48-page FA Cup special. It was a little disappointing however to find that

THE REAL TRACTOR BOYS

this had been achieved by re-producing a number of photographs of top flight football venues and FA cup winners with the reader being invited to guess the answers of the ridiculously easy questions. There was very little text to read, not even the thoughts of the manager.

The strangest feature however is entitled 'Mystical Mandy'. Mystical Mandy is a busty blond who predicts the final score of the game. Today, Mystical Mandy thought that Town would beat Wanderers 2-1! Her prediction was spot on so far.

As the teams ran back out on to the pitch little did I know that I was about to witness the best goal of my Suffolk adventure so far. Almost directly from kick off, the tricky Camillo Douglas (yes, him again) found himself with the ball with space just inside the Stowmarket half. The ball had bounced kindly and he just hit it goal bound. In what seemed like slow motion, the ball sweetly lobbed the Stowmarket keeper to give the away team the lead again.

Douglas thus preceded the run the length of the pitch whilst stripping his shirt off. I have never quite understood why scoring a goal provokes players to take their clothes off however he was obviously delighted and I do not blame him one bit. The inevitable booking he received from the referee was quite humorous as Douglas simply held his shirt out, back to front to reveal his number 10.

Stowmarket began to force the game and scored a deserved equaliser in the 80th minute. Substitute Andy Moyes drove the ball home from the edge of the penalty area. No more goals ensured the right result between two determined teams and meant that a replay would be required to settle who would progress to the next round of the FA Cup. Mandy may claim to be mystical but she was wrong on this occasion.

STOWMARKET TOWN 2 – 2 IPSWICH WANDERERS
Attendance 87 @ Greens Meadow

EXTRA TIME – The rematch was played on the Wednesday and it was Wanderers who won convincingly 2-0 in front of 116 spectators. So Ipswich Wanderers lived to fight another day in the World's oldest, most famous cup competition – not for long though as they were knocked out by Cornard United in the next round.

CLUB INFO

ADDRESS – Stowmarket Town FC, Greens Meadow, Bury Road, STOWMARKET Suffolk IP14 1JQ
WEBSITE – www.stowmarkettownfc.co.uk
ADMISSION - £4.00 + £1.00 programme
MILES TO & FROM CLUB – 25 miles

HALF TIME

Monday 1st September 2008 was transfer deadline day. On this day, Europe's top football clubs scrap around trying to sign or sell players before the strike of midnight. After this time no more transfers are permitted until the transfer window opens on the 1st January.

The window was introduced by the world's governing body, FIFA, in the 2002-03 season to stop teams trading players throughout the season. To be honest I have never really understood why this was a problem and many football managers are against the window system as it creates a panic buying situation. It also means that the smaller clubs are really restricted during the season if they suffer from a number of injuries and are unable to strengthen their squad.

It does however create quite an exciting day. Sky Sports have really taken to the event and spend the whole day following the deals being conducted across the country, with roving reporters outside the grounds, as players arrive in cars with limo-tinted windows. It makes great viewing.

The last transfer deadline day was on the 31st January 2008. During the day, reports were stating that Jermain Defoe would be moving from Spurs to Portsmouth to replace the departed Benjani, who was on his way to Manchester City. City desperately needed to strengthen the team up front and whilst I was not sure Benjani was the answer, I still kept in touch with the news all day. The deal was still unconcluded by 10pm, so I decided to stay up until the transfer was confirmed. Midnight came and went and whilst Defoe had signed for Pompey there was still no news from Eastlands.

As 1am approached I decided that I had to go to bed and get some sleep, confident that everything would be sorted out by the morning. After all, many deals are not actually announced until the early hours, despite the paperwork being submitted to the FA before the midnight deadline.

The following day, I immediately turned on the TV in bed and selected page 302 on BBC teletext. Much to my amazement the

THE REAL TRACTOR BOYS

deal had not gone through and Benjani was not a City player, however the story did not end there as it appeared from reports that the move may still go through! We will probably never really know the truth surrounding the deal, however it transpired that Portsmouth had received a call from City at 11.55pm advising them that the paperwork to sign Benjani had been submitted to the FA. Portsmouth then proceeded to register the deal for Defoe. Portsmouth were then contacted by the FA at 12.15am and told that they had not received any paperwork from City for Benjani.

Apparently Benjani had arrived too late in Manchester for a medical. A number of reports stated that he had fallen asleep at the airport and missed two flights. Others stated that he was so shocked and distressed that Portsmouth wanted to sell him that he stalled on getting up north. Whatever the reason, City did not have time to perform a medical on the Zimbabwean and tried to back out of the deal. After an FA investigation and subsequent negotiations, Benjani did sign for City on February 5th but for a reduced fee of £3.75million with a further payment of £3.75 million if he played 75 games.

I thought that the whole deal had been quite exciting and intriguing however nothing could have prepared me for Monday 1st September 2008. City had had an odd start to season. I had watched the opening game away to Aston Villa and the team had been woeful, losing 4-2. There were rumours abound regarding the financial situation of the club after the controversial owner and former Thai prime minister, Thaksin Shinawatra had skipped bail in Bangkok and was seeking asylum in London. His assets of more than £800million had been frozen and reports suggested that former chairman, John Wardle had bailed the club out in the summer by paying the players wages.

Former Manchester United and Barcelona striker Mark Hughes had replaced Sven-Goran Erikkson as manager and whilst a couple of new players had been signed, the season kicked off with City looking weak in a lot of departments.

Despite the rumours of a cash flow problem, City completed the £6million signing of Belgian international, Vincent Kompany from Hamburg and looked a different team the following weekend beating West Ham 3-0, a game that I watched in a bar

THE REAL TRACTOR BOYS

in Portugal. Then in an amazing move the club re-signed Shaun Wright-Phillips from Chelsea in a deal worth a reported £9million.

The following weekend City played away at Sunderland and Wright-Phillips scored twice on his debut as the team won 3-0 again. The same day, the signings of Argentinean defender Pablo Zabaleta from Spanish club Espanyol, and Brazilian Glauber Berti from German side Nuremburg were announced. Where was the money suddenly coming from?

The answer soon became apparent. At about 10am on transfer deadline day I received a text from my Dad advising that the club was being taken over by a consortium called Abu Dhabi United – effectively the Abu Dhabi royal family. They had obviously been in negotiations with the club and it was them who had paid for the recent acquisitions and they would not stop there! Rumours started to circulate the news channels, websites and message boards that City were making a late bid to sign the Spurs striker Dimitar Berbatov, who had appeared to be destined for Man United all summer.

I do not think that my mobile phone has worked so hard during one 12-hour period. With Dad off work, he was glued to Sky Sports and was updating me every 20 minutes. Bid for Berbatov accepted. Berbatov flying to Manchester but picked up by Alex Ferguson. Mark Hughes expecting to speak to Berbatov. Berbatov seen at Old Trafford. City making bids for Spain's David Villa and Germany's Mario Gomez. By the time I got home I had already decided that I would be up until gone midnight again watching events unfold.

At about 10pm the race to sign the Bulgarian, Berbatov seemed to be all but over. United had got him despite our late efforts. And then a new story broke. City had bid a British transfer record £32.5million for Real Madrid's striker Robinho. The small Brazilian had been courted by Chelsea all summer and I could not help think we would be beaten to a player again. But at 11.58pm Sky's reporter outside Eastlands (now dubbed Middle Eastlands) confirmed that City had got their man. Robinho had signed for Manchester City! I could not believe it! The next day, press reports suggested that City's new owner would be chasing Christano Ronaldo, Cesc Fabregas, Fernando Torres and Kaka in the January window

What was going on? And what relevance does this all have to my tour of Suffolk's non-league football grounds?

Well, Dad was convinced that this season could be special for City. He had tried to persuade me to get a Season Ticket in the summer but I declined, stating that I did not have the money or the time to do all of the traveling required. As a result of the excitement, Dad raised the subject again and in fact went further to state that he was going to get a Season Ticket and he would help me out financially, so excitedly, I decided to join him. I was going to do something I thought I would never be able to do – be a Manchester City Season Ticket holder. However this would be bound to affect my tour of Suffolk. I was determined to continue and complete the tour however it would take longer, and mean more midweek night games. And what would Gemma say?

Only time would tell.

THE REAL TRACTOR BOYS

HAVERHILL ROVERS v ELY CITY

FA VASE 1st QUALIFYING ROUND Saturday 6th September 2008

After all of the excitement regarding Manchester City and getting the season tickets, the following weekend was an international one, meaning that England were playing and there were no Premier League or Championship games. My first game as a City season ticket holder would start a week later on Saturday 13th September at home to Chelsea, so I decided that I better make the most of a spare Saturday while I could.

THE REAL TRACTOR BOYS

And Haverhill seemed a good place to get done and out of the way, as I did not fancy heading over there midweek. With a population of 22000, Haverhill is closer to Cambridge and Stanstead Airport than Ipswich and is in the far South-West corner of Suffolk, just minutes from Cambridgeshire and Essex. It is a 45-mile journey and with no obvious direct route, with the AA route planner suggesting a trip via Bury St Edmunds.

Despite the extra miles required to get to Haverhill, I was looking forward to visiting the club and their ground, Hamlet Croft. I had been warned by the brilliant football grounds magazine, 'Groundtastic' that Hamlet Croft was close to being sold off and a new ground being built. The magazine had stated that the closure was foreseeable and a well worth a visit.

The visit of Ely City in the 1st Qualifying Round of the FA Vase seemed an ideal fixture. The FA Vase is a competition restricted to clubs from Step 5 of the football pyramid and below. The final is played at Wembley and Suffolk clubs have been especially successful in recent years, with AFC Sudbury making three consecutive finals between 2002 to 2005, unfortunately losing on all three occasions. Last season another Suffolk club, Lowestoft Town, made it to the final but they too lost. A local derby with Long Melford FC awaited Haverhill Rovers if they could deal with Ely plus £800 prize money from the FA.

The weather forecasters were promising that an Indian Summer was just around the corner however it looked far from likely, as I drove through shower after shower on the A14, heading for Haverhill. The AA route planner predicted a journey time of 1 hr and 15 minutes, so I had set off at about 1.45pm hoping that I would be a little quicker than the computer suggested.

Luckily the rain had stopped when I arrived. Hamlet Croft is one of those funny grounds where you can drive straight in and pay at the gate from the car window. A kind of drive-thru turnstile.

There is plenty of space to park inside the ground. Hamlet Croft has a very open feel about it, generally something I am not keen on, but this endangered ground has a redeeming quality. Three sides of the pitch are simply open but one side is bordered with a steep bank. At the top of the bank is a single track concrete concourse. On the other side of the track is the main stand, and it

THE REAL TRACTOR BOYS

is a pretty good one, capable of seating 200. It is constructed from wood and steel. There are no individual seats just large wooden steps so you just pick your spot and park your rear. As a result of the steep bank, the view of the pitch has to be one of the best in the league. However, whilst viewing the game at height provides a better perspective of the game, it does remove you from the side of the pitch and the feeling of being part of the game, which for me is the whole reason for watching non-league.

To one side of the stand is the club house and changing rooms and to the other is a snack bar. Unfortunately there is no covered terracing. It therefore seems even more incredible that a ground record attendance of 1730 crammed into the ground a couple of seasons ago for an FA Cup 4th Qualifying Round versus Aldershot Town.

Haverhill Rovers play in the Eastern Counties League Premier Division after winning promotion from Division One, the same year they faced Aldershot. This season had not got off to the best of starts with just one win, one draw and four defeats under their belts, including a 6-0 thrashing at Kirkley & Pakefield. This poor

The entrance to Hamlet Croft, home of Haverhill Rovers FC

start had left the club one from bottom in the league table. Perhaps a break from the league in the form of this cup tie would provide the kick start they needed.

The opposition, Ely City, also play in the Eastern Counties Premier Division and had a slightly better start to the season. The Cambridgeshire club also possesses one of the most picturesque grounds in the Eastern League, with views across open fields to Ely Cathedral in the distance. I had previously visited their Unwin Ground, en route to Northampton a couple of years ago, and had watched a highly entertaining game against Ipswich's Whitton United and can recommend a visit.

As I walked around the pitch towards the main stand at Haverhill's Hamlet Croft, I could hear the sound of a drum and some singing. Ely City had bought some singing support with them in the form of eight or so, 15 year olds. They were absolutely tremendous and sang throughout the game. It did seem odd though that one of their chants was "Come on City"! Surely just mentioning City must mean that we were watching a game at Vauxhall Conference (sorry Blue Square Premier) level at least. In fact, Ely is the third smallest city in England (after Wells in Somerset and the City Of London – which doesn't really count!) with a population of just over 15,000. It qualifies as a city as a result of the aforementioned cathedral.

I picked my spot on the main stand steps just in time for kick off. Ely dominated the first half, spurred on by the singing support, but failed to make it count. The Haverhill goalkeeper, Ed Campbell, was in fine form and well deserved being awarded 'Man of the Match' after the game.

At half time I decided to get a cup of tea and have a listen to my iPod. I am far from being a techno-phobe but neither do I rush out to get the latest gadget. Gemma got me an iPod for Christmas and up until then I had not realised how much I wanted one! Yes, you can store loads of songs, but for me the greatest advantage is the world of pod casts. Available free of charge, you simply find a pod cast that takes your fancy and download it from your computer. If you really take a liking to something you can subscribe (still free) and every-time an edition is released, it simply appears on your PC ready to be transferred to your iPod.

The main stand overlooking the pitch.

There are many pod casts available to suit all tastes. The BBC produces highlight packages of their regular radio shows so every week 'The Russell Brand Show' and 'The Adam & Joe Show' find themselves onto my iPod, and I guess the comedy genre is the most popular but there are also some excellent football shows. Many clubs produce their own weekly editions, but some of my other regular listens include the BBC's 'World Football Phone In' and The Guardian's 'Football Weekly' presented by James Richardson, of Channel 4's Football Italia fame. There are also some lesser known, independently produced shows available and on the day in question I tried out the 'Football Ramble' for the first time.

The 'Football Ramble' is simply a group of mates who love football, having a chat (one of whom sounds remarkably like Steve Claridge). However, they know their stuff and it is pretty funny so well worth a listen. The episode that I had downloaded was recorded before the Man City takeover and one of the presenters made the comment that with the reported financial doom at City, Mark Hughes decision to take the job was one of the worst in the history of football! He retracted his statement the following week.

Back to the match and Haverhill were much better in the second half, but the score remained 0-0. With a replay looking likely and my desire to get back home to watch the England match in the evening, I started to make my way to the exit with about ten minutes to go until the final whistle. I hung around at the corner of the ground wondering when to actually go, and would I miss a vital goal. With five minutes left on the clock I decided to get going as it had started raining again. In the 86th minute, Haverhill scored the winning goal – just a minute after I had left. Typical! According to the brilliant club website Craig Cutts scored for the home side. Never leave early!

HAVERHILL ROVERS 1 – 0 ELY CITY *Attendance 103 @ Hamlet Croft*

EXTRA TIME – Haverhill's delight did not last long. They were knocked out of the competition in the next round by local rivals, Long Melford 1-0, just two weeks later.

CLUB INFO

ADDRESS – Haverhill Rovers FC, Hamlet Croft, Hamlet Road, HAVERHILL Suffolk CB9 8EH
WEBSITE – www.hamletcroft.co.uk
ADMISSION - £4.00 + £1.00 programme
MILES TO & FROM CLUB – 87.8 miles

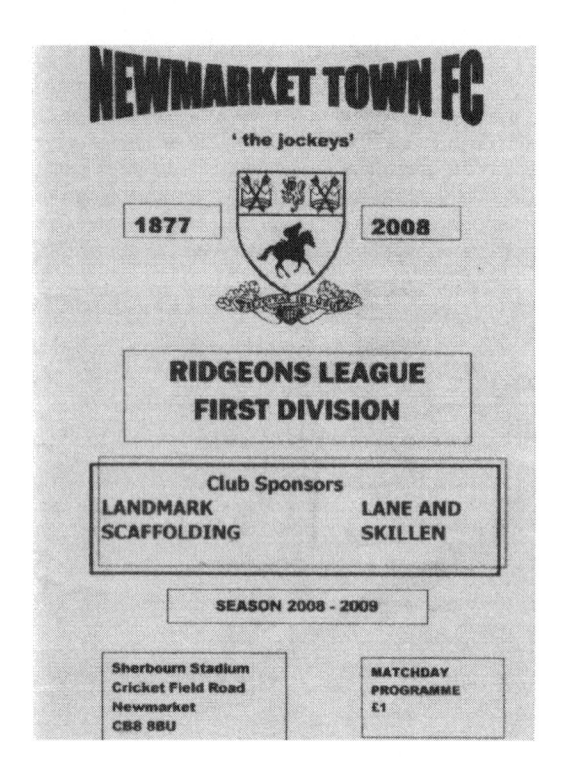

NEWMARKET TOWN v MARCH TOWN UNITED

FA VASE 2nd QUALIFYING ROUND Saturday 20th September 2008

While Haverhill were losing to Long Melford, I had decided to watch Newmarket Town in the next round of the FA Vase. With Manchester City facing Portsmouth on the Sunday, I decided to stop off at Newmarket Town en route to Northampton on the Saturday. I had visited the ground before in similar circumstances so nothing was really new but it was a nice day and I always enjoy a match.

THE REAL TRACTOR BOYS

Like Haverhill, Newmarket is only just in Suffolk. In fact it is tucked into an enclave with only a small strip connecting the town to the county. In years gone by, the town was part of Cambridgeshire and in the 1972 Local Government Bill it was proposed (and supported by the town) that Newmarket would return to Cambridgeshire, however this notion was overturned by the government and it remains in Suffolk. Having said that, twice in recent weeks both Sky Sports and the BBC have stated that the town is in Cambridgeshire.

Newmarket is famous for one thing – horse racing. Racing in the town dates back to the 12th century and it is now the home of British horse racing. It is reported that up to 2500 horses live in Newmarket, compared to the human population of 15,000. There are 70 licensed trainers and over 60 stud farms in and around the town. And driving through Newmarket you cannot help but notice all of the horse tracks and crossing points. It is really worth a visit.

Newmarket Town FC was founded in 1877 and currently play in the Eastern Counties League Division One along with today's

The entrance to the Sherbourn Stadium, home of Newmarket Town.

61

THE REAL TRACTOR BOYS

The main stand at The Sherbourn Stadium.

opponents, March Town United – a club definitely in Cambridgeshire. Newmarket Town play at the Sherbourn Stadium, the sponsored name of Cricket Field Road. I arrived just before kick off, in time to take a seat in the impressive main stand. The 200-seater stand straddles the half way line and is raised high enough to accommodate the dugouts in front. These dugouts are no longer is use as a year or so ago, new UPVC dugouts were constructed on the opposite side of the pitch. There is also a small section of wooden covered terrace between the two new dugouts.

To the right of the main stand is a small physiotherapy room, followed by the brick-built clubhouse, housing the changing rooms, snack kiosk and bar. The walkway in front of the clubhouse is covered and there is also a section of covered terrace in the corner of the pitch, next to the club house. The rest of the ground is open with trees behind each goal and another couple of pitches beyond the new dugouts.

Newmarket Town were relegated from the Premier Division at the end of last season but their bid to bounce straight back had started well. The club went into this match as joint leaders of the division, having won six, drawn one and remaining unbeaten. March Town United were mid table. On the face of it, the £900 prize money from the FA looked as good as won.

THE REAL TRACTOR BOYS

Both teams played really well. The home team combined good football ethics with strength and power to boot. I was really impressed with a lad playing on the left wing, especially in the second half. March Town United had an incredibly young line up. The majority of the players appeared to be under 20-years old and it was their lack of experience and strength that eventually told. Half time arrived with no goals, but Newmarket powered through and in the second half knocked in three.

It was a glorious day and really quite warm sitting in the sun. The view from the stand at Newmarket is very good although obviously not as high as Haverhill Rovers. With a nice little ground and positive signs on the pitch it is a shame the attendance of 73 for this FA Vase tie was the lowest I had encountered so far. And whilst moaning I must mention the Newmarket Town website and match day programme.

Nothing appears to have happened on the website since the end of last season, with the last recorded result a report dating back to 3 March 2008. It is now expected by most people that every football club has an up-to-date and informative website. Many clubs have embraced the internet and provide loads of fantastic information. As a roaming non-league fan I always check fixtures on club websites, especially if the weather is looking dodgy. It is therefore really frustrating when a website exists for a club but is not maintained.

The match day programme is the worst I have come across. Advances in printing mean that many clubs produce amazing publications, with colour covers, loads of stuff inside, even if sometimes they feature too many advertisements. The Newmarket Town programme is like stepping back in to the 1970s. In fact, it reminds me of one of the programmes from a game my Dad might have featured in. I confess that the programme gives me all of the information I really need, however it is leagues behind their local rivals. I do appreciate that things like websites and programmes are maintained by volunteers and I apologise if I have upset anyone, but they are a long way behind the competition.

The Football Association uses the Vase to try out new initiatives and this fixture was no exception.

One of the beauties of non-league football is the ability to have a pint of beer whilst watching the game. In fact, the clubs rely on the sale of alcohol throughout the game as an important source of income. In their wisdom the governing body has decided to ban spectators from enjoying a pint of their favourite tipple at pitch side. I really cannot see the point. In many years of watching non- league games I have never seen any trouble and whilst some fans get a little tipsy (the Ipswich Wanderers' Ultras being one group) they never cause any harm and generally improve the atmosphere with a bit of singing.

Another initiative is for the players to line up and then shake each others hands before the kick off, in the same way the professional players do in the Premier League. I suppose there is nothing wrong with this however all of the players looked uncomfortable doing so and I must admit I always like the way the two teams sprint out of the changing rooms, heading for their end of the pitch. This line up business seems to dilute this moment of passion and I doubt the players have more respect for one another as a result.

I also noted from the FA website that a couple of Vase fixtures had been chosen for a new style of match decider, if the game ended in a draw. Rather than a penalty shoot out at the end of a stalemate, players would take shots at goal from the centre spot, I assume with no keeper in goal! This would be very entertaining, however as far as I am aware none of the chosen games ended up in a draw.

I really enjoyed the game at Newmarket and ordinarily I would say that a non-league game can be as pleasurable as a top flight fixture. However the following day I travelled to Manchester to watch my second game as a season ticket holder, and witnessed City beat Portsmouth 6-0! Overall though, I had watched two games with 9 goals and none conceded, in one weekend. I doubt that will happen very often

NEWMARKET TOWN 3 – 0 MARCH TOWN UNITED
Attendance 73 @ Sherbourn Stadium

EXTRA TIME – Once again I had seen a team win an FA Vase fixture only for them to go out in the very next round. A couple of weeks later, Newmarket Town lost 4-2 away to Norfolk side,

Dereham Town.

CLUB INFO

ADDRESS – Newmarket Town FC, Sherbourn Stadium, Town Ground, Cricket Field Road, NEWMARKET Suffolk CB8 8BT
WEBSITE– www.webteams.co.uk/newmarkettownfc/ (not updated since March 2008
ADMISSION - £4.00 + £1.00 programme
MILES TO & FROM CLUB – 83.8 mile

THE REAL TRACTOR BOYS

WALSHAM-LE-WILLOWS v WIVENHOE TOWN

RIDGEONS EASTERN COUNTIES LEAGUE PREMIER DIVISION Saturday 11th October 2008

Another round of international fixtures meant that there was no trip to Manchester, so a great opportunity to bag another Suffolk non-league football ground. The weather forecast was good and Gemma was up for another match, so I decided it was a great time to get out into the countryside and visit a really rural ground.

The exotically named Walsham-le-Willows, is situated half way between Bury St Edmunds and Diss and has a population of just over 1000. It boasts two pubs and a delightful church. When I first moved to Ipswich I worked briefly for Mid-Suffolk District Council as a Visiting Officer for the benefits department (one of the worst jobs I have ever had) and Walsham was in my patch. I therefore knew roughly how to get to the village but had no recollection of a football ground.

Unfortunately, I only realised that I had misplaced my Suffolk atlas at ten past two on the day of the game, knowing full well that trying to find a non-league football ground in even the smallest of villages can be almost impossible. I resorted to a quick search on the internet to find the location of the ground and then set off on a frantic dash to cover the 26 miles from home. Typically the ground was really easy to find (but I suppose it always is when you know where to go) but just goes to show that the AA route finder is not too accurate on journey times as they predicted it would take 54 minutes and we made it in just under 40!

Situated in Summer Road, the Sports Ground is a fantastic little spot. Surrounded on three sides by established trees and woodland, Summer Road felt like a football oasis in the middle of rural Suffolk. The autumnal sun pierced through the trees and it was incredibly warm for mid October. There is a small car park immediately upon entering the ground and admission is paid to a man housed in what can only be described as a partially glazed shed. To the left is smart new clubhouse housing the changing rooms, toilets and bar. The pitch is bordered by a concrete path and metal railings with neat mesh netting covering the gap between the railings and the ground.

The main stand is constructed from concrete and metal and seats 100 spectators in line with the centre spot. The team dugouts are situated either side of the main stand. This is my favourite way of doing things. I hate it when the dugouts are opposite the main stand as it isolates the majority of spectators from the team management. There is a small area of covered terrace behind the goal, farthest from the clubhouse corner.

The vista from our seats in the stand was fantastic, especially with the sun beaming down on our faces. To our left we could see smoke rising into the treetops from a BBQ next to the clubhouse.

The main stand at Summer Road, Walsham-le-Willows

For some reason the whole scene reminded me of a German campsite I had once stayed at. The smell was fantastic and I decided that a half time burger was definitely on the agenda.

Football at this level in Walsham-le-Willows is in its infancy. The club played its first game in the Eastern Counties League Division One in the 2004-05 season and amazingly finished 4th and also played in a cup final at Portman Road. In 2005-06 they entered the FA Cup for the first time in the club's history. After just two seasons in division one, the club won promotion to the Premier League. After struggling last season in the Eastern Counties top flight, the club had started this season really well and went in to this fixture in 6th position, having won four, drawn four and lost just two games so far.

In opposition were Wivenhoe Town, from Essex. The club had started the season well and was sat in fourth position following relegation from the Ryman League the previous summer. There had been a lot of comings and goings from the Wivenhoe squad

THE REAL TRACTOR BOYS

during the close season, with manager Richard Carter making wholesale changes in preparation for the new league.

I had hardly had a chance to flick through the informative match day programme (only 50p) before the game kicked off. Right from the start, the visitors looked the stronger of the two teams and it was not soon before they took a deserved 1-0 lead. Walsham were really struggling to get a foothold in the game and it was therefore quite a shock when they equalised, just before half time, with a rare attack on the Wivenhoe goal.

It was during the first half that I saw one of the most heartwarming sites at any match I have ever been to. Just after kick off, an elderly gentleman and his young grandson sat down in front of us. Despite his advancing years you could tell he had been a strong man but with his grandson it was also obvious that he was a caring and loving grandfather. His grandson, probably about 7 years old, wore a little hooded top and jeans and he sat with his legs dangling off the edge of the seat. He adored his grandfather and kept asking him questions about the game. Lots of kids go to non-league games, but rarely watch the match, with most of them playing with a ball behind the stand, and there is nothing wrong with that however this lad's interest and thirst for knowledge was delightful – even if he did think Wivenhoe in their green and yellow strip were Norwich City.

It was therefore with great disgust that I have to report an incident in the second half of the game. Wivenhoe were pressing for another goal and had made all of their substitutions in an effort to force the issue. A Wivenhoe player was then grounded with an injury that looked like it could be serious. The Wivenhoe goalkeeper called over to the bench and declared that a sub might be required. At the top of his voice and with total disregard for anyone who might be in earshot, someone replied "We've used them all you c**t!"

This outburst was met with a number of moans and sighs from the main stand. I could feel the anger of the grandfather in front of me, knowing that his young grandson was about to ask "What does that mean Grandad?" I was pleased to see that the linesman felt it appropriate to warn the offending person of his language, and I would have liked him to be sent off. Please understand that I am not adverse to colourful language being spoken when watching the working man's sport but it really was totally unnecessary.

From that moment on, my desire for Walsham to steal an undeserved winner multiplied. Unfortunately there is no justice in the world and Wivenhoe soon scored their second goal of the game. Oddly, the goal seemed to spark Walsham in to life and they started to exert themselves on the game for the first time. It was at this point that the second moment of controversy occurred off the pitch.

A Walsham player was fouled approaching the opposition's penalty area. The referee allowed the game to play on, with Walsham retaining possession, and looking like a goal scoring opportunity might occur. Alas, the chance never materialised and Wivenhoe won the ball back. An elderly spectator behind us called out to the referee. "Hey ref, that should have been a free kick!"
"But he gave you the advantage instead of the free kick." Came the response from a Wivenhoe fan.
The Walsham fan replied "But it didn't turn out to be an advantage so we should have the free kick!"
Now raising his voice, the away spectator responded, "But you can't have both! It doesn't work that way. How ridiculous. I've never heard such rubbish!"
The Walsham gent was extremely angry with that and stated "Well it's my ground and I can say what I like so...up yours!"
"Up yours too!" came the response. And with that the argument ended, but for one moment I thought I was going to have to split up two retired gentlemen scrapping in a crowd of 69! I had not heard the phrase 'up yours' used for a long time and whilst its connotation is obviously offensive, it has to be a lot more palatable then the vocabulary earlier.

Much to my annoyance, Wivenhoe won the game and we made our way out of the ground to our car that was parked on the verge. I guess it was more relief than annoyance for one of the spectators, that the game had finally ended. One of the home team's girlfriends had watched the whole game from her car. Despite the vehicle being suitably parked facing the pitch, she spent most of the game reading magazines, and I assume counting down the minutes.

THE REAL TRACTOR BOYS

The view from the main stand at Summer Road, Walsham-le-Willows

Non-league WAGs are an amusing bunch. They come out in force in the summer, wearing sunglasses and supporting the team for whom their bloke has just signed for. Socialising with the other WAGs and eating chips are usually the main activities with watching the game in third position however this all ends towards mid October and they disappear into hibernation until the spring returns, the following year.

WALSHAM-LE-WILLOWS 1 – 2 WIVENHOE TOWN
Attendance 69 @ Summer Road

EXTRA TIME – Just 19 days later, despite Wivenhoe winning seven consecutive games, manager Richard Carter was sacked for operating beyond the agreed budget and failing to provide promised funds. Reports stated that the club owed players wages in excess of £30,000. A week later it was reported that Carter had offered £60,000 to buy the club! Wivenhoe lost all but two of their players but former West Ham Utd and Liverpool full back, Julian Dicks came to the rescue and took over as manager. In January 2009 he signed former team mate and Ipswich Town player Stuart Slater to play for Wivenhoe. The 40-year old winger was born in Sudbury, in Suffolk.

CLUB INFO

ADDRESS – Walsham-le-Willows FC, Walsham Sports Club Ground, Summer Road, Walsham-le-Willows, BURY ST EDMUNDS Suffolk IP31 3A
WEBSITE – www.leaguelineup.com/walshamlewillowsfc
ADMISSION - £4.00 + 50p programme
MILES TO & FROMCLUB– 57.6 miles

WHITTON UNITED v LOWESTOFT TOWN

THE L.B. SUFFOLK F.A. PREMIER CUP 1st ROUND Tuesday 14th October 2008

Whitton United are my most local club. They play at the King George V Playing Fields, which are located next to the main road into Ipswich, having left the A14 at the commonly known 'Asda' exit. The whole ground and pitch is visible from the road and on Saturday afternoons, motorists stuck in traffic can watch the game. And it is for this reason I was not looking forward to watching Whitton United.

THE REAL TRACTOR BOYS

The ground is nothing to get excited about and having seen all it has to offer almost every day whilst driving past, I had no feeling of discovery or intrigue to get me motivated. I was therefore careful to choose the best fixture I could find and a visit from table topping, and well supported, Lowestoft Town suggested that at least I would see some goals. The fixture was in the first round of the Suffolk Premier Cup, a competition that has provoked a lot of interest locally in the last couple of seasons. Why? Well, Ipswich Town enters their reserve team into the competition and this means that everyone wants to play them, for two main reasons. Firstly, the teams get to pit their wits against professionals and secondly, plenty of Ipswich Town fans attend the game, which considerably boosts the attendance and therefore the coffers of the club.

Whitton United have had a presence in Ipswich dating back to the late 1800s, but only have documented history from 1926 when they played in the same league as Ipswich Town. Oddly, despite the clubs lack of facilities and kudos they have had a number of links with famous players. The club's main sponsor is West Ham United's winger, Kieron Dyer, who grew up on the Whitton estate. Previous managers include former Norwich City, Newcastle United and Tottenham Hotspur winger Ruel Fox and Plymouth Argyle and Bury player Ronnie Mauge. In fact the current management team of Gary Thompson and Neil Gregory are both former professional players.

It is a short five minute drive to the ground from my house and I should really have walked, but it was showing signs of rain so I chickened out. The car park was pretty busy with a number of away fans expected and a little old man directed me where to park. Entrance was the standard £5 with an excellent programme for a further pound. I was immediately greeted by a young girl handing out a magazine, produced by the Suffolk FA, all about respect and a free 'One game, one community' pin badge. I must admit that I just put the badge in my pocket (not that I don't agree with the principles) however it soon found itself adorned to my jacket after I saw Mark Hughes wearing one in a post-match interview.

To the right of the turnstile is a small brick built tea and burger bar. Standing facing away from the burger bar, the pitch slopes up hill toward the main road, with just a huge wire mesh fence

THE REAL TRACTOR BOYS

separating the ground from the passing traffic. On the right hand side of the pitch are the usual towering conifer trees and the team dugouts. On the left hand side, about half way up the pitch, is a small wooden covered terrace that can house about 50 people at a push. It simply looks like a large bus shelter. And that is it, apart from the clubhouse in the car park, which is apparently called 'the shed' locally. The fact that it was a night game and the floodlights were on made the situation better because you could not immediately see the road, only when cars passed.

The lack of seats and terracing was an obvious disappointment however something felt good. The club usually only attracts attendances of about 30-40 spectators so the boost to 78, with a number of vocal and replica-strip wearing away fans was helping the atmosphere. I tried to think what else was doing it for me. The match day programme is certainly deserved of a better supported club and features a lovely picture of the ground on the cover. It is informative and interesting and a credit to the club. The greeting from the chap on the turnstile certainly helped – "Really good to see you." He said. No-one has ever said that before.

And so, kick off arrived and I really wanted Whitton to belie their league position of 2nd bottom, with just one league win to date, and give high fliers Lowestoft Town a game. Unlikely considering the away team were unbeaten - granted! My worst fears were confirmed when Lowestoft took the lead in the 8th minute, when Russell Stock volleyed in a Bradley Hough cross. I could not help to feel that the flood gates would now open and Whitton would be humiliated. Amazingly though, the home side got a goal back just three minutes later, with Duane Wright scoring. Lowestoft regained the lead just before the half hour when Bradley Hough headed home a Carl Poppy cross. But Whitton stuck at it and scored a deserved equaliser, just before half time with Clarke getting on the score sheet.

Having spent the whole of half time queuing for a cup of tea, I had only just taken up my spot along the side of the pitch when the players returned for the second half. Shortly after the kick off, Lowestoft were forced to shuffle their players, after Poppy left the field with an injury. They took time to settle and Whitton capitalised when Williams scored, to put them in front for the first time in the match. The away side did not panic though and

75

within 10 minutes they were level again with Jaime Godbold getting in on the goals. And Godbold scored his second goal of the game, another ten minutes later to give Lowestoft a 4-3 lead. And that is how the score stayed. Whitton had done themselves proud and made a real game of, what on paper, had looked like an easy fixture for their visitors.

The bumper crowd for the visit of the league leaders had caused chaos in the car park. I managed to complete what seemed like a 10-point turn in order to head back the way I had entered the car park, only to find my exit completely blocked by other parked vehicles. I figured that there must be another way out and perhaps there is a track around the club house like a little one-way circuit, towards the exit. I reversed all the way back through the car park, against the tide of spectators returning to their own cars. I reached the club house only to find that, much to my embarrassment, there was no other exit! And so I headed back the other way to the amusement of onlookers. Thankfully the exit had since cleared and I was able to escape.

WHITTON UNITED 3 – 4 LOWESTOFT TOWN
Attendance 78 @ King George V Fields

EXTRA TIME. – Despite Whitton's performances on the pitch improving, things behind the scenes were not so great. The manager, Gary Thompson, resigned a few weeks later to become the Assistant Manager at Tiptree United (in Essex). The credit crunch had also put the club's plans to build a brand new stadium on hold. Then came the major shock news – the club resigned from the league, stating that they were unable to satisfy their fixtures due to a lack of finance and players. All of the team's results were wiped from the records, as if they never happened. I felt gutted for all of the people concerned and hope that the club makes a real go of it next season, wherever that may be.

CLUB INFO

ADDRESS – Whitton United FC, King George V Playing Fields, Old Norwich Road, Whitton, IPSWICH Suffolk IP1 6LE
WEBSITE – www.whittonutdfc.co.uk
ADMISSION - £4.00 + £1.00 programme
MILES TO & FROM CLUB – 1.6 miles

WOODBRIDGE TOWN v AFC SUDBURY

THE SUFFOLK F.A. PREMIER CUP 1st ROUND Wednesday 15th October 2008

Eager to make the most of the Suffolk Cup fixtures, I decided to watch another game the night after the fantastic feast of football I witnessed at Whitton United. Woodbridge Town are in the Eastern Counties League Premier Division and the visit of AFC Sudbury from a league higher would be a real test.

Woodbridge is a small town eight miles east of Ipswich. It is a pretty little town, which lies on the River Deben, and has a delightful harbour with the Tide Mill, a working water mill, as the focal point. The town has a population of about 10,000, amongst who is the actor Brian Capron, who played the murderer, Richard Hillman, in Coronation Street. The town is also the birthplace of Brian Eno from Roxy Music and Charlie Simpson from the teen rock band, Busted

Woodbridge Town Football Club was founded in 1885. The first recorded match played by the club was the 10-0 defeat of Ipswich team, St Helens. The club also holds the distinction of winning the first Suffolk Senior Cup in 1886, beating Ipswich Town 3-1 at Portman Road, at the third time of asking after a 2-2 draw and a 0-0 draw.

Woodbridge Town joined the Eastern Counties League Division One in 1989 and moved to their current home at Notcutts Park in September 1990, with a friendly game against an Arsenal XI which attracted a 3,000 strong crowd in the opening game. In 2004, former Ipswich Town and Colchester United player, Mick Stockwell took over as manager of Woodbridge Town. Stockwell, who was born in Chelmsford, played over 500 games for *The Tractor Boys* between 1985 and 2000. Mick oversaw the implementation of a successful youth development policy at the club and a number of good young players have progressed through the ranks at Notcutts Park. In 2007, Stockwell left the club by mutual consent and he is now a pundit on local radio.

It takes about 25 minutes for me to cross Ipswich and through the sprawling Kesgrave conurbation to reach Woodbridge. The anticipation builds as you approach the town on the A12, with the floodlights illuminating the sky. Notcutts Park is a smart, modern, non-league football ground. Access is gained through a delightful brick-built turnstile incorporated into the main building. The main stand provides the only covered viewing area for fans and rather uniquely accommodates standing spectators (at the rear) and seated spectators (at the front) - about 200 people in total. The rest of the ground is open. The club appears to be one of the most successful commercially. The majority of the pitch perimeter is adorned with advertising hoardings and the excellent website features links to all of the club sponsors. The match day programme is free with admission and is one of the best in the region for player information.

THE REAL TRACTOR BOYS

On the previous Saturday, when I was at Walsham-le-Willows, the club had run a promotion in conjunction with the local newspaper, *The Evening Star*. The paper printed a voucher that offered readers admission to the league game versus Wisbech Town, plus half a pint of Fosters lager or John Smiths bitter for just £2.50 (or £1.00 for senior citizens!). The promotion certainly worked as a bumper crowd of 435 attended, compared to 162 the week before. A great example of how clubs can increase their attendances with a bit of imagination. Unfortunately Woodbridge lost the game 3-1 and perhaps missed the opportunity to convert some of the new faces to visit again and I must admit I was expecting a bigger crowd for this cup fixture, against one of the most supported clubs in the county. However, England were playing Belarus in a World Cup Qualifier on television, so a number of people probably decided to stay at home in the warm.

The game started in a lively fashion and AFC Sudbury's intent was clear. They had named a strong line up and were looking too powerful for a young Woodbridge team. It took AFC 30 minutes to open the scoring with a strike from Kevin Hawes, a recent signing from Maldon Town, in Essex. Hawes added a second goal just before the break to make the score 2-0. At half time I decided to move from the club house side of the pitch, to view the game from near the team dug outs, on the opposite side. I had had time to read the free magazine issued by the Suffolk Football Association at the Whitton game the night before. The general theme of the publication was all about respect and the FA claims that 8,000 referees quit the game last year. 846 grassroots games were abandoned last season due to unacceptable behaviour by players or fans. Love them or hate them, without the referee there is no game.

I do not think the Woodbridge management team had read the magazine yet. For the ten minutes I stood by their technical area, they hurled abuse at the referee. According to them, everything that went wrong for Woodbridge was the official's fault and nothing to do with players making mistakes or poor coaching. I had the same view of every decision made and I personally thought that the referee, Nick Cooper, had a very good game. The late, great, Brian Clough famously insisted that his players respected all match officials and one of his former players, Stuart Pearce, recently said in an interview in *The Independent*, "I've been brought up under Brian Clough to keep my mouth shut. All decisions are going to be balanced over a season. If you don't think refs are going to make any mistakes just look at your own performance as a player or manager and know you can't get decisions right all the time. The same things applies to them – it's physically impossible with the pace of the games nowadays." Why can this attitude not be adopted by everyone in football, especially by clubs that specialise in developing young players?

I believe that the vast majority of all match officials perform to the best of their ability and make decisions on what they see. They try their best to be fair and consistent but now and again they will make mistakes. I fail to see how hurling abuse at the referee is going to help your team at all. I must admit that if I was a referee and had received the sort of abuse that some teams dish out, I would think twice before awarding them a penalty. Likewise I might be more forgiving to the team that had shown me respect. It is to the credit of the officials that they remain fair throughout games because I do not think I could do it!

The second half was a tight affair and remained scoreless until the 85th minute when AFC Sudbury's James Rowe scored a third goal for the Southern League side. In the closing minutes Woodbridge's determined efforts paid off, as they scored two goals in quick succession to make for an exciting finish to the game, but Sudbury had already done enough to win the game and go on to face Mildenhall Town in the next round.

WOODBRIDGE TOWN 2 – 3 AFC SUDBURY *Attendance 114 @ Notcutts Park*

EXTRA TIME – The manager of Woodbridge Town resigned from his position at the end of January, after the club had slipped to second bottom of the league. He was replaced by 31 year old, Christian Appleford

CLUB INFO
ADDRESS – Woodbridge Town FC, Notcutts Park, Fynn Road, WOODBRIDGE Suffolk IP12 4D
WEBSITE – www.woodbridgetownfc.co.uk
ADMISSION - £5.00 + free programme
MILES TO & FROM CLUB – 17.8 miles

THE REAL TRACTOR BOYS

BRANTHAM ATHLETIC v LONG MELFORD

*RIDGEONS EASTERN COUNTIES LEAGUE DIVISION ONE –
Tuesday 11th November 2008*

Having watched Manchester City self destruct again versus Tottenham, on the Sunday, followed by a horrendous drive home through pouring rain, floods, and closed roads, it was to my own surprise that I was checking out the local non-league fixtures less than 48 hours later!

I had written in my diary that high flying Leiston were playing Ipswich Town in the Suffolk FA Premier Cup, however the fixture

THE REAL TRACTOR BOYS

was cancelled at Tuesday lunchtime due to a waterlogged pitch. I started to check out the other games that were still on, despite the weather conditions, and I was left to choose between two Ridgeons Eastern Counties League Division One fixtures. Debenham LC were playing Ipswich Wanderers (who I have already reported on twice in this book) and Brantham Athletic versus Long Melford. I was keen to visit Brantham for a number of reasons but the fact that Long Melford had just signed an ex-Ipswich Wanderers' player, Rene Swann, who I was keen to see him play again, swung the Brantham game in my favour – and it is closer to home.

I first watched Rene Swann a couple of years ago, when I first started watching Ipswich Wanderers. He is a pretty accomplished striker at this level and scored a stunning 74 goals over three seasons with the Humber Doucey Lane club. Last season he signed for Whitton United but only played a couple of games before quitting, citing family and work commitments. Considering he is only in his late 20s I was surprised at his decision and therefore delighted that he signed for Long Melford at the end of October. He scored twice on his debut in Melford's last game, a 4-2 win away at March Town United.

Brantham is a small village on the Suffolk and Essex border, close to the small town of Manningtree, in between Ipswich and Colchester. I was recently talking to a friend of mine from Northampton (not a fan of football) who had recently visited the area and stayed in nearby Dedham. He had passed through Brantham and was astonished to learn that the village possessed a football club that charged an admission. "But it's just a road with a few houses" he said. I could not have put it better myself.

The football club was founded in 1887 and originally joined the Eastern Counties League in 1978. Their best performance was in the 1982-83 season when they finished 4th in the league and played VS Rugby in the 5th round of the FA Vase - a narrow 1-0 defeat in front of a record 1700 crowd. Unfortunately the success was short-lived and by 1995 the club dropped out of the Eastern Counties League, into the Ipswich & Suffolk League. Last season however, the club won promotion back to the 'big time' and I was eager to watch them play, especially as they had received quite a bit of press coverage during the close season.

THE REAL TRACTOR BOYS

To begin with, the former AFC Sudbury manager, Mark Morsley joined the club as Chief Executive. His company MJM Financial Management became the club's main sponsor and he set about bringing in some proven, quality players. Unfortunately, by the time I visited to watch Brantham, Morsley had left to take over as manager of Harwich & Parkeston FC. Obviously the lure of hands on management was too much to resist.

I set off for Brantham at about 7.15pm for the short 10 mile journey. I had passed the ground just a couple of weeks earlier, en route to Manningtree to view a car for sale, so I thought I knew how to get there. Unfortunately, I missed the exit off the A12 and found myself on the outskirts of Colchester with just five minutes until kick off. Thus ensued a frantic cross country drive with me simply following my nose until I stumbled across the village. Thankfully I had only missed five minutes of the game and managed to pick up the last match day programme, included in the admission price of £5.00.

Considering the club had only just returned to the Eastern Counties League, I was shocked to read in *Groundtastic* magazine that the club had won an auction to buy a 500-seater stand from Colchester United, when they vacated Layer Road to their brand new stadium. I had been told by someone, who had played against Brantham, that they already had a stand, so why did they need all of these seats? They obviously had big plans!

The ground is positioned behind the village's leisure centre and admission is via a turnstile, housed in a shed. The left hand side of the pitch is completely open with an adjacent cricket pitch. I overheard a Long Melford fan, question how the club can get away with no barrier or path surrounding the pitch, which I must agree, I thought was a minimum ground requirement at this level. The situation is the same behind the far goal end, which was also totally open.

The right hand side of pitch features a metal barrier and concrete path together with brick-built dugouts. Behind these is a wooden stand featuring bench seating that can apparently accommodate 200 spectators. A redundant portacabin is positioned next to the stand. It is at the goal end nearest to the turnstile where the new stand from Colchester is being erected. Having never visited Layer Road, I imagined the stand being pretty old, with blue and white seats featuring CUFC emblazoned across it. Alas it is a fairly new metal structure, which I assume occupied a gap between older structures at Colchester United, put up when they found themselves in the Championship. The stand was still closed off to the public and was positioned in the left hand corner, but only appeared to feature 100 or so seats so I guess that there is more to come!

Obviously the game had started when I arrived, so I made my way past the old wooden stand and stood near the away team's dugout. It was funny watching Long Melford again in conditions so different to the balmy summer's evening when I watched them in a pre-season friendly in August. The rather weak Brantham floodlights only just lit the pitch, which was covered in fallen autumn leaves and rather boggy. Both teams appeared to be very young with most of the players still teenagers. Unfortunately, my much anticipating viewing of Rene Swann was not to be as there was no sign of him, so I guess he still had work commitments.

Brantham came into this game after having their previous game abandoned. The club had been losing 2-1 away at table-topping Newmarket Town when one of their players, Marlon North suffered a serious leg injury. An ambulance had to attend and after consulting the two teams, the referee decided to abandon the game. To make things worse, North was playing his first game after two years out through injury.

The game started well, with Brantham looking the most likely to score. I was immediately struck by the Long Melford management team. In appearance, one chap reminded me of the character 'Smithy' in BBC TVs 'Gavin & Stacey'. It just so happened that the linesman was operating the half of the pitch directly in front of the away team's dugout. And 'Smithy' had a lot to say to the officials. As his team started to drift out of the game it was apparently the officials fault and not his own team's failings. The linesman chose not to entertain any of 'Smithy's' criticism of the officials. Finally 'Smithy' declared to anyone in ear shot "He can't speak – that's the problem!" To be honest, I had exactly the same view of the game as the Long Melford management team and I could not see a problem with any decision.

I was therefore shocked when another bloke bellowed at the top of his voice "You're a fucking cheat ref!" The outburst was all the more shocking considering his relative silence to date. Now if I was the referee I would have sent him off. To accuse the match officials of cheating is unprofessional and unforgivable. The very next day, the Newcastle United manager, Joe Kinnear, was being asked by the FA to explain his comments regarding a referee, when he had stated that some of the decisions were "Mickey Mouse". This seems small fry compared to the outburst from the Long Melford bench!

The home team were growing in stature and could have scored a couple of times but for fine saves by the Long Melford goalkeeper. But he could not stop Brantham forever, and they took the lead in the 32nd minute.

At half time I headed up to the club house with the first stop being the toilets. The men's loo turned out to be opposite the away changing room and for some reason the club officials had forgot to unlock the door, so the team were queuing up outside. By the time I came out of the toilet, the team had made it into the changing room and I could easily hear the manager giving them a piece of his mind. I headed for the long queue outside the refreshment hatch. Whilst waiting for my cup of tea I noted with interest that different food was available for different fixtures. Fans would be treated to a Cajun chicken baguette at the forthcoming fixture with Gorleston and I must admit I was tempted by the BAFC Burger, but opted for a Kit Kat instead.

The rollicking dished out by the Long Melford management team failed miserably as within 10 minutes of the kick off, Brantham were winning 3-0. It was at this stage that the referee did make a strange decision. The ball went out of play for a Brantham corner, and very obviously so, however the referee awarded Long Melford a throw in. Now I did not hear the Melford management team moaning then!

BRANTHAM ATHLETIC 3 – 0 LONG MELFORD
Attendance 70 @ Brantham Leisure Centre

EXTRA TIME – By the end of December things had not improved for Long Melford and the manager was moved upstairs (if there is an upstairs at a non-league club) to the position of General Manager.

THE REAL TRACTOR BOYS

CLUB INFO

ADDRESS – Brantham Athletic FC, Brantham Leisure Centre, New Village, Brantham, MANNINGTREE Suffolk CO11 1R
WEBSITE – www.branthamathletic.co.uk
ADMISSION - £4.00 + £1.00 programme
MILES TO & FROM CLUB – 22.4 miles

DEBENHAM LC v GORLESTON

FIRST DIVISION KNOCK-OUT CUP 1st ROUND – Tuesday 18th November 2008

Now I must admit that a game at Debenham LC was another fixture that I was not looking forward to. A few months earlier I was in the area and decided to check out the ground. The LC in Debenham's name stands for 'Leisure Centre' and the ground is simply behind the leisure centre - unsurprisingly. In fact, I managed to gain access to the ground via a public footpath that runs alongside the leisure centre. It is simply a pitch surrounded by metal railings with sporadic advertising hoardings, floodlights

THE REAL TRACTOR BOYS

and a small pre-fabricated 100-seater main stand. No terracing, no cover, no outside snack bar and therefore no character.

I suppose it is not surprising though as the club is the youngest in the county. Founded in 1991 as Debenham Angels, the team progressed quickly through the minor leagues, winning five promotions to join the Eastern Counties League in 2005. It was at this time that the club changed their name. Debenham LC entered the FA Vase for the first time in 2006-07 and the FA Cup for the first time the following season. It therefore makes it incredible to think that a ground record 1,026 watched the team take on AFC Wimbledon in September 2007 in their first ever campaign.

Debenham is a scenic village in rural mid-Suffolk with a population of about 4,000. It is a 16 mile journey from my house but at least I knew where I was going this time. In their previous game Debenham LC had lost 1-0 to high flying Leiston, in the FA Vase and it was Leiston that occupied my most immediate thoughts as I got in the car. BBC Radio Suffolk were providing live commentary on Leiston's FA Cup 1st round reply, away in Lancashire against Fleetwood Town. Leiston's cup achievements this season had been nothing short of fantastic. The adventure had started back in August with a win against Blackstones FC, in the Extra Preliminary Round. That was followed by wins against March Town United, Cornard United, Carshalton Athletic, Coalville Town and finally Blue Square Conference side Lewes. If Manchester City beat that many teams in the cup they would be in the final!

The BBC radio presenters were obviously discussing local non-league football and whether the county could support a club higher up the non-league pyramid. They considered the possibility that AFC Sudbury, Lowestoft Town or Leiston could perhaps survive in higher leagues but one of the presenters made a valid point about match attendances. He stated that Ipswich Town have approximately 15,000 season ticket holders, of which 1,000 of those travel to away games as well. So why don't the remaining 14,000 get out and watch some local non-league football when Ipswich are away from home. I tend to agree. But I think the net can be cast further than that. I know numerous so-called football fans who never watch a game live in the flesh and just sit in front of the television. That said, it was recently reported that attendances in the Eastern Counties League are up by 5% on last season and the league is, by far, the most watched in the United Kingdom at step five.

I arrived at Debenham leisure centre just a couple of minutes before kick off. I headed for the turnstile at the side of the building but was a bit concerned that it was all very gloomy with no lights on. I then noticed a sign instructing me to obtain entrance via the main leisure centre reception. I walked through the main doors. A couple of tracksuit clad women were paying for their squash court at the desk. I headed into the bar and then through some sliding glazed doors as I could see the football pitch floodlit beyond. It was then that I realised I had not paid an admission fee and more importantly I did not have a match day programme. After glancing around, I noticed two official looking chaps leaning on a table, amending team sheets. I asked where I should pay. One of the gentlemen advised me that I should pay at the main reception but that I might as well not bother now that I was in! He obviously did not appreciate my need for a programme. I paid the £4 admission plus £1 for the all important programme and headed back out to the pitch. The guy who I had spoken to before looked at me as if I was some sort of idiot as I passed by him again. "But you didn't have to pay!" he remarked.

It was a cold night but a nice little crowd had turned up for this re-arranged fixture (the game had previously been abandoned at the beginning of the month after 39 minutes due to fog). Despite the young age of the club and the lack of character of the ground, they make a lovely little programme that does help to give the club an identity, as does the yellow kit and nickname of 'the hornets'.

The programme features a number of match reports, league tables, fixture lists and the all important brief history of the opposition and pen pictures of the players. Bearing in mind that Debenham were founded in 1991, it was with amazement that I read that Gorleston were founded way back in 1684, 'making them one of Norfolk's oldest football clubs'. Well, if they really were established 324 years ago they would be the oldest club in the World, let alone Norfolk, and would be older than football itself. A quick check on the internet at home suggests the date printed in the club history should be 1887.

I was immediately impressed with the quality of both teams considering neither are setting Division One alight this season. But it was the home team looking that little bit more dangerous and they deservedly took the lead towards the end of the first half. Needing to visit the toilet, I headed back inside at halftime. The loos were signposted as in the main part of the leisure centre. Unfortunately the first gents I arrived at were locked but a notice on the door advised that further gents toilets were located upstairs. So upstairs I went and found myself looking over a game of energetic five-a-side football. It was at this point I started to feel a little over dressed. I was kitted out for a cold night's football viewing, and had my large coat, scarf, wooly hat and thermal motorcycle trousers on. This feeling of being a little overdressed was dramatically heightened as I came face to face with a naked man in the toilets at the end of the corridor, which were also the main leisure centre changing rooms!

Having enjoyed a warming cup of tea after my changing room encounter, I headed back out to the pitch. The BBC Radio Suffolk coverage of the Leiston game was being relayed via the public address system. When the Debenham game kicked off for the second half I continued listening to the Leiston game on a pocket radio I had taken with me. Unfortunately Leiston were 1-0 down. Meanwhile back to the game I was watching and Debenham were really stamping their authority on the game. I was especially impressed with Debenham's Warren Taylor-Holt, who had a really good game and reminded me of the former Manchester City winger Darren Huckerby in both style and appearance. It was a superb cross by Taylor-Holt that was met by the club's top scorer, Stuart Jopling to make the score 2-0. The game was then sealed by James Heathcote to send Debenham through to the next round.

Unfortunately the batteries in my pocket radio had died after about half an hour. By the time I was back in the car, Leiston were 2-0 down and out of the FA Cup. Heartache for the smallest club left in the World's most famous cup competition but a plucky effort and probably the best time to bow out of the tournament to concentrate on the competitions that they can realistically win.

DEBENHAM LC 3 – 0 GORLESTON *Attendance 66 @ Maitlands*

CLUB INFO

ADDRESS – Debenham LC FC, Maitlands, Debenham Leisure Centre, Gracechurch Street, Debenham, STOWMARKET Suffolk IP14 6BL
WEBSITE – www.debenhamfc.tripod.com
ADMISSION - £4.00 + £1.00 programme (but could have been free if I had just kept walking!)
MILES TO & FROM CLUB – 27.6 miles

THE REAL TRACTOR BOYS

LEISTON v IPSWICH TOWN

LB SUFFOLK FA PREMIER CUP Tuesday 25th November 2008

A week after listening to Leiston FC do Suffolk proud, I got to watch them myself for the first time and it was another big game for the club. Having won away at Newmarket Town in the first round, Leiston were rewarded with the glamour tie at home to Ipswich Town, albeit the reserves, in the Suffolk Premier Cup.

I was pretty amazed that I was even considering watching this game. The previous Saturday I had watched Manchester City win 3-0 against a troubled Arsenal. All had been well until I arrived

THE REAL TRACTOR BOYS

home at 11pm and strained my neck reaching for a cup of tea. Sounds unlikely, but those readers who have suffered from bad backs and necks will understand that it is the stupid little things that are the straws to break camel's backs...or my neck! I was in absolute agony and could not even lie down. I spent the whole of Saturday night sitting up in the living room and the following Sunday was not much better. Luckily by Monday it was getting better and Tuesday's fixture was back on the cards.

As Suffolk's only professional football club, Ipswich Town have huge support throughout the county and fans generally turn out even if it is only the reserves playing. Unfortunately on the night in question the first team were playing away at Birmingham City, in the Championship, so that meant the caliber of players available for the trip to Leiston would be reduced however despite that, and the dreadful weather, a good crowd turned up at Victory Road.

I almost did not though. Once again I had under estimated the time it would take me to drive the 25 miles from home. My dash up the A12 was also hindered when I hit road works. Not only was one lane shut and traffic lights in operation, the guys working decided it was the ideal time to close the whole road and move various bits of machinery around was just as I arrived. After what seemed like 15 minutes of waiting, (but more probably 5) I flirted with the idea of giving up and going home but decided to give it a go anyway - especially as a story in the local *Evening Star* newspaper had hinted that the former Real Madrid and Bolton Wanderers midfielder, Ivan Campo might play.

I eventually made it to the ground and paid the increased admittance of £6, just after the game had kicked off. Unfortunately, there was no sign of Campo. Apparently the drop from the Bernabeu to Victory Road was one step too far. There were however a number of faces I did recognise. Although I had never seen Leiston play I did know a number of their players. Goalkeeper Jaime Stannard (regarding as the best keeper in the league), defender Mark Goldfinch and midfielder Marc Lowe had all previously played for Ipswich Wanderers when I watched them play a number of games a couple of years ago. Lowe's dad, Mick, is the physio for Leiston and he used to work in the same building as me. In fact, at a Christmas party a couple of years ago, after having a few too many beers, I pestered Mick for ages to tell me how much his son got paid at Wanderers. Mick was hammered too, but would not tell me a thing!

The Leiston team also featured Shane Wardley and Brett Girling who I had seen play for AFC Sudbury. Unfortunately, the most famous Leiston player, Tes Bramble, was injured however I did see him watching the game from the warmth of the club house. I had seen Tes at the start of my tour with his brother Titus at the Ipswich Wanderers v Antigua & Barbuda game. Leiston were also missing another striker, Daniel Cunningham. The highly rated young prospect had recently been arrested in connection with drugs offences. Cunningham had signed for Leiston in late 2007 having previously played for Bury Town and AFC Sudbury.

For Ipswich Town I recognised Jaime Peters, Jordan Rhodes and Ed Upson, who all played in the pre-season friendly at Bury Town. I think the rest of the players were from the youth academy. Finally, and perhaps most worryingly I recognised the referee, Nick Cooper. After a couple of minutes of scanning every corner of my memory I remembered he was in charge of the Woodbridge Town v AFC Sudbury fixture in the previous round of the cup. This was getting sad!

I had parked a couple of streets away, as the club's website warned that the car park was waterlogged and had enjoyed a short walk to the ground. I love the feeling of going to a night game. Just head for the floodlights, piercing through the darkened skies, the muffled sound of the public address system and the strange mixed aroma of burgers and Deep Heat!

Having passed through the turnstile you find yourself almost parallel with the half way line. To the left, the club house stretches to cover almost half the pitch. To the right is a good area of covered, standing terrace that is ever so slightly tiered. Behind the goal to the right was open with a burger van ready to cater for the higher than average attendance. Behind the opposite goal it is also open but with a portacabin housing the club shop and another snack bar. On the opposite side of the pitch is the main grandstand that seats about 150 spectators. Either side of the stand are the dugouts.

Despite to poor weather, the pitch looked in good shape. The game had already kicked off and the home team looked

THE REAL TRACTOR BOYS

impressive. It became immediately apparent that Leiston's team of experienced non-league players were keen to show the Ipswich Town youngsters that they could play too. I suspect a couple of the Leiston players were also looking to show the Ipswich Town reserve team boss, Chris Kiwomya, that they could still make it as a professional. It occurred to me that a number of the young Ipswich academy players would be new to playing in this sort of environment, usually playing in empty stadiums or behind closed doors and it took them time to adapt.

But adapt they did and in the 20th minute, midfielder Ed Upson scored for the professionals with a fine drive. Half time arrived and the score was 1-0 to the away team. I had a cup of tea, that was the temperature of lava, from the burger van and then popped into the club house to use the toilet. Inside there was a large television screen showing the Champions League fixture between Villareal and Manchester United. A workmate had managed to obtain a ticket. He did not even have a valid passport until the previous Friday and his convoluted journey which involved a budget flight and connecting coach and train trips, led me to wander whether he had actually made it or not.

Leiston came out in the second half with real purpose, determined not to crash out of two cups in the space of seven days. However, after a period of sustained Leiston pressure, Ipswich scored their second goal of the night in typical, professional, fashion. It was a break against the run of play and after real heroics by Jaime Stannard in the Leiston goal, Jordan Rhodes slotted the ball into the net.

It was all but over and the home crowd became a little frustrated. After a couple of beers the fans got louder and louder and started to focus on the referee and the Ipswich players. One Leiston fan shouted to the referee after a pretty innocuous tackle on a Leiston player, "Why are you protecting them ref? Be a man and stand up to them! Book him!" "That's right", I thought, "Be a man, referee, and give in to pressure from the crowd, even though you know you're right!"

The joke amongst the home fans soon became to shout to the Ipswich players; "That's why you're in the reserves" when they misplaced a pass, or "You won't be signing a new contract" when a shot went wide. It was pretty tame stuff compared to the usual non-league banter but it was interesting to see the reaction of the young lads. They would look up in shock and try and see who it was in the crowd who could have said such a thing! They simply were not used to hearing such comments.

They did, however, have the last laugh and scored a third goal just two minutes from time, sealing a comprehensive victory and take their place in to the semi-finals, and face the winners of Needham Market v Walsham-Le-Willows early next year.

LEISTON 0 – 3 IPSWICH TOWN *Attendance 253 @ Victory Road*

EXTRA TIME - My workmate did make it to Villareal, but it took him an extra day than expected to get home!

CLUB INFO

ADDRESS – Leiston FC, LTAA, Victory Road, LEISTON Suffolk IP16 4DQ
WEBSITE – www.leistonfc.co.uk
ADMISSION - £6.00 + £1.00 programme
MILES TO & FROM CLUB – 52 miles

CORNARD UNITED v DEBENHAM LC

RIDGEONS EASTERN COUNTIES LEAGUE DIVISION ONE
Friday 5th December 2008

As I neared the end of my tour I started to think about where I wanted to watch my last game. I had four clubs to go – Cornard United, Mildenhall Town, Kirkley & Pakefield and finally Lowestoft Town. I thought it would be good to finish with a big game and in Suffolk they do not get much bigger than the Lowestoft derby, between Town and their near rivals, Kirkley & Pakefield. The game is traditionally played on Boxing Day and the attendance likely to be in the region of 1,000. Luckily for me, this year the game would be on Saturday 27th December as I had an appointment in Manchester to watch the visit of Hull City on the 26th!

So the question was, could I do the other three before Christmas, as well as watch Man City? Initially it was not looking good but then some fixtures were altered and everything slotted in to place. Watching Kirkley & Pakefield was not a major problem as they had a couple of midweek games, although I was not really looking forward to the hour's journey up the A12 after a day at work. Mildenhall then announced a midweek home fixture against Histon Reserves on Tuesday 9th December. And finally Cornard United moved one of their home games to a Friday night! Fingers crossed everything would go OK, and my grand finale would be at the big match in Lowestoft at the end of December.

Friday seemed an odd day to play until I realised that their close neighbours, AFC Sudbury were playing a big game against Bury Town on the Saturday, so in an effort to get some sort of a crowd I guess they opted to play the night before. I became aware of the fixture because of the Ridgeons Eastern Counties league website however no kick off time was stated. Unfortunately Cornard United's website was last updated in 2007 so no help there. The Debenham LC website had also not been updated since before my visit to watch them a couple of weeks ago, so another blank. I started to wonder if the game was actually happening. Cornard United are one of the worst supported clubs with one game, this season, watched by just 25 lowly spectators. The thought occurred to me that there might be more people on the pitch than

THE REAL TRACTOR BOYS

those watching.

My mind was put at rest the day before the game, when the local newspaper featured a couple of lines referring to the fixture, stating the match was expected to be played, despite recent poor weather. In fact the club had not cancelled a game in the last ten years! Kick off was 8pm. Cornard is a village on the outskirts of Sudbury, approximately 20 miles from home. The journey generally takes half an hour but I did not know where the ground was and also had to stop en -route to make an emergency toilet roll purchase, so left home at 7pm.

I arrived in Cornard at about 7.45pm and pulled over to take a quick look at the map I had printed out earlier that day. I felt around under my coat, on the passenger seat but it was not there. Moving the coat and switching on the interior light did not make the map magically appear. I must have left it at home. I searched my photographic memory and tried to remember where the ground was. I recalled that it was somewhere between the road I had just arrived on and another one leaving the village towards Bures. It was also on a small country lane just outside of the village, near a cricket ground. How many roads can there be? Surely I would find it? But after two dead ends and one full circle I was none the wiser. The game had now kicked off, perhaps the programmes would all be sold, and it had started raining. To make things worse, I knew I needed to waste more time topping up the credit on my phone before I could call home for directions. My wife confirmed that the map had been left by the front door. Having worked for a couple of years in Cornard she knew the area and asked which road I was on. She would be able to direct me from there. Unfortunately I had no idea where I was with anger and annoyance blurring my logic and common sense. After a few minutes she got me sorted out and I found the country lane I needed so I thanked her and hung up.

I headed up what I thought was the correct road but started to get concerned when the road narrowed to a single track. It was one of those roads with grass growing in the middle. This did not feel right. I continued up the hill for another couple of minutes but suddenly a car appeared in front of me, coming in the opposite direction. There did not appear to be anywhere for either car to immediately pull over and give way. The car facing me, a Peugeot, was not budging so I had no alternative but to reverse back. I had only purchased the car I was driving a month or so a go - a Citroen C4. I had noticed that the C4 featured just one small reverse light, low down inset to the bumper. I had not really thought this would ever be a problem but as a consequence the solo light did nothing to illuminate the road behind me. I could not see a thing.

A steep bank bordered the left hand side of the road and what could have been ditch on the right. Living in a street lit town, it is so easy forget to how dark it gets at night. In front of the car was obviously fine but to the sides and rear of the car the thick blackness obscured tree stumps, rocks, ditches and numerous other hazards that kept popping into my head. Despite moving ever so slowly I kept veering onto the verge and with every metre the rear screen became more and more misted.

After what seemed like five miles of reversing, there was still no sign of the end of the road. Another quick glance forwards and I noticed that the oncoming Peugeot had taken the gamble of pulling onto the banked verge and was at quite an angle. There appeared to be enough space for me to proceed forward and pass. There was not much room and just as I thought I was clear my offside wheel clipped the bank and pushed the Citroen right, towards the Peugeot. With my heart in my mouth, I missed the waiting car by the slimmest of margins and made it through. Now sweating, I headed up to the top of the hill. At the peak I reached a crossroads with no obvious clue as to the proper road ahead. I decided to go straight on but it soon became apparent that I was no longer on the public road but on a farm track. After negotiating a blind (in total darkness) three point turn I got myself back on the road. After another couple of miles I found myself back on the main Bures road again. After all of that I was not on the right road at all!

It was now half past eight and there was no point in even trying to find the ground. I kept seeing what appeared to be the haze of floodlights but I gave up trying to find out where on earth it was. I decided to head home. I had been at risk of doing a 'Cornard' before but had found grounds just in time. Finally after visiting 16 grounds spread across Suffolk I had failed to find one. I would have to go home and rethink my plans. I was desperate to make the Lowestoft derby fixture my last game but it was now in the balance because of my poor preparation. I arrived home over two hours after setting off, with a Citroen that looked like it had just completed a stage of the RAC Rally. At least I had got the toilet roll!

For the record 52 people did manage to find the ground and watch Cornard United lose 2-1 to Debenham LC. It should have been 53 but I would have to visit Cornard again.

MILDENHALL TOWN v HISTON RESERVES

RIDGEONS EASTERN COUNTIES LEAGUE DIVISION ONE
Tuesday 9th December 2008

To maintain my target of finishing the tour at Lowestoft on the 27th December, I had set myself up with a tough week, with two games on consecutive days in two different corners of the county. First stop was Mildenhall, a 74-mile round trip from home.

In the north west of Suffolk, the market town of Mildenhall has a population of just under 10,000 and is perhaps most famous for the large Royal Air Force base which is home to the United States

Air Force refueling division. It is not uncommon to see reregistered American cars cruising the streets and even the football club's main sponsor is 'EUROUSA', an international moving company.

My journey to Mildenhall takes in the A14 to Bury St Edmunds where I then pick up the B676 to the 'five ways roundabout', a junction on the A11. Whenever I approach this roundabout I am reminded of the journey we used to make when I was a child, from Northampton to visit family in Norfolk. The 'five ways roundabout' always meant that we were almost in Norfolk and from there it would be another hour until we arrived at our grandparents. It seemed like an endless journey at that age, especially if you were the one having to sit in the boot of the Volvo estate, looking out backwards!

The town's football club has been in continuous existence for 110 years, being founded in 1898. They were founding members of the Eastern Counties League first division in 1988 but despite this long history, the silverware cupboards are pretty bare with the only major trophy coming in 1996 when they won the Cambridgeshire Invitation Cup - ironic considering they are obviously based in Suffolk.

Mildenhall Town have been in the Premier Division since 1998 and this was also when they moved into their current, community funded, football ground adjoining the local leisure centre. The area where the club is based also seems to be the number one spot for local teenagers to hang around. I had previously been to watch 'The Hall' in a pre-season friendly on a balmy summer's night and the amount of kids about led me to wander whether anyone between the ages of 13 and 18 were at home, or anywhere else to that matter, within a 10-mile radius.

The car park of the leisure centre was proving not be as popular with the kids in early December however. I had already had to scrape ice from my windscreen before setting off from home at 6.30pm and I was in serious fear that the game would be cancelled. The lawn at home already had a touch of frost and I had checked various websites and internet forums a number of times before setting off to see if that game was still on.

Entrance to the ground is beyond the leisure centre and after passing through the turnstile you find yourself at the corner of the pitch, with one of the goals to your left. Straight ahead is a section of covered terrace stretching approximately a third of the pitch. After the terrace is the clubhouse with a window serving drinks and snacks. Past the brick building is a small covered stand which backs onto the changing rooms. There are only 50 seats and they are pretty low down and whilst it is pretty neat it seems like a missed opportunity when a more substantial stand could have been erected in this space.

The rest of the ground is open to the elements with the usual conifer trees behind each goal and the dugouts on the opposite side of the pitch. There appears to be a substantial slope to the pitch and it did not look in the best of conditions, the wear and tear of winter beginning to take its toll.

Pre-season optimism for Mildenhall had given way to mid-table realism with the club sitting in 9th position in the league before this game. The opposition, Histon Reserves were seven points behind in 13th spot however they do deserve a special mention for two reasons. The first being the meteoric rise of Histon FC in recent years. As recently as 2000 the Histon first team were playing in the Eastern Counties Premier Division and at the time of writing they are sitting in second position of the Blue Square Premier (more commonly known as the Conference) - the top tier of non-league football in England. Just a few weeks ago Histon knocked Leeds United out of the FA Cup, a game televised on ITV, and were looking forward to a third round fixture against Swansea City. So, while Histon had moved up the football pyramid, their reserve team had climbed the divisions too as if attached by a piece of rope.

And that is the second point worth raising. Many fans (and I include myself in this) feel that higher club's reserve teams playing in the ECL has a somewhat demeaning effect. In the ECL Premier Division there are three reserves teams (the other two being King's Lynn Reserves and CRC, an amalgamated Cambridge United & Cambridge City reserve team). These teams are occupying top flight spots at the expense of 'actual' football clubs who are stuck down in the First Division or out of the league altogether. I appreciate that the best teams win and move up the leagues however these reserve outfits do not really have the feel of proper clubs and I think it is a shame they are allowed to compete in the ECL, as I would much rather see teams such as Great Yarmouth or Halstead Town in the top flight.

The cold weather was the top subject amongst the hardy souls who were brave enough to venture out and watch this game. That plus the sending off of their goalkeeper Shaun Marshall in their last game against Woodbridge Town! Marshall had been adjudged to bring down an advancing Woodbridge striker and a penalty awarded. Marshall had then seen red apparently and went nose to nose with the referee for which he was sent off. The general consensus amongst the spectators was that he would get a lengthy ban from the Suffolk FA, possibly a couple of months, therefore effectively ended his time at the club.

Shaun Marshall's replacement between the sticks for this fixture was a young keeper called Josh Pope and he had a commanding start to the game until he dropped the ball in the 20th minute, allowing Histon to take an early lead. The score remained 1-0 at half time and whilst it was a hard fought contest I must admit I had spent a lot of the opening 45 minutes trying to work out what a couple of the guys behind me were talking about. "So is it just six of us on Saturday?" the first chap said. "No, didn't you hear?" came the response "Stuart's pipe in the loft burst while he was on holiday and the house is flooded. Might just be five of us."
"That's an embarrassment" the first man continued "I wish people wouldn't say they were up for something if they're not actually going to do it!"

I assumed it must be some sort of six-a-side football team but as the conversation developed, the plot thickened. The first man was still moaning "How can you book in somewhere as a society and then just five people turn up? What sort of society is that?" That was exactly what I was thinking. I hope it was some sort of real ale appreciation club...if not, I am not sure I want to know!

In the second half Histon really stamped their authority on the game scoring three more goals, with the last two in the final 10 minutes to earn a well deserved, comprehensive victory.

On the way home I began to get rather frustrated with drivers with their rear fog lights on despite it not being foggy. Do these drivers not realise that their lights are on despite it clearly showing on the dashboard? Or do they simply want to stand out like a lighthouse, dazzling the driver behind? Either way, it gets so difficult to see when these cars are braking because the fog lights are so bright, especially on older cars. I followed an old Rover 600 that dazzled me all the way from Mildenhall to Bury St Edmunds. The road is a mixture of 30mph speed limits in villages and then 60mph outside. This Rover stuck to 45mph all the way. It really scares me that some drivers seem absolutely oblivious to everything else around them. Sorry - moan over!

MILDENHALL TOWN 0 – 4 HISTON RESERVES
Attendance 89 @ Recreation Way

EXTRA TIME – The Mildenhall Town goalkeeper Shaun Marshall was banned for six months after a Suffolk FA panel ruled that he had assaulted a match referee!

CLUB INFO

ADDRESS – Mildenhall Town FC, Recreation Way, MILDENHALL Suffolk IP28 7HG
WEBSITE – www.freewebs.com/mildenhalltownfc
ADMISSION - £5.00 + £1.00 programme
MILES TO & FROM CLUB – 74.8 miles

THE REAL TRACTOR BOYS

KIRKLEY & PAKEFIELD v DEREHAM TOWN

RIDGEONS EASTERN COUNTIES PREMIER LEAGUE
Wednesday 10th December 2008

For the second night in a row I was on the road, stretching the boundaries of Suffolk to the limits. It is a 100-mile round trip from my home to Lowestoft, the home of Kirkley & Pakefield FC and therefore I set off at 6.15pm, eager not to do another 'Cornard'!

Lowestoft is the most easterly town in the United Kingdom and with a population of just under 60,000, it is the second largest town in the county. It is therefore not surprising that the town boast two Eastern Counties League Premier Division clubs and interest in non-league football has boomed in recent years.

The town is split by Lake Lothing, a saltwater lake which links to the North Sea through Lowestoft harbour. The districts of Kirkley and Pakefield are both south of the lake. There are records of a football club bearing the name of Kirkley FC dating back to 1886 when the *Lowestoft Weekly Press* reported a series of games against East Suffolk FC. The two teams eventually merged to become Lowestoft FC. According to the informative and award winning match programme the name of Kirkley FC then appeared again in 1890, however to find a direct path through history to the current day we have to fast forward to 1978, when Brooke Marine FC applied to change their name to Kirkley FC. Oddly, Lowestoft Town still 'owned' the name of Kirkley and it is still incorporated in to the club rules; therefore the name of Kirkley United was adopted for the 1978-79 season.

Over the next couple of decades the club rose through the leagues until, in 2003 they won promotion to the Eastern Counties League. In 2005 they moved up to the Premier Division to join their north Lowestoft rivals. On Boxing Day 2005 a ground record crowd of 1,124 fans watched the Lowestoft derby. In 2007 the club merged with Pakefield Boys FC to become Kirkley & Pakefield FC.

The club moved to Walmer Road in the 1980s on the site of the former Lowestoft golf course. A lot of improvements have taken place in recent years with the help of the Football Foundation and the facilities are now very impressive. I arrived in perfect time for the 7.45pm kick off although it had just started raining as I passed through the turnstile. The pitch looked absolutely superb; ten times better than Mildenhall's the night before. There are a couple of modern buildings housing the changing rooms and match officials room. The old golf course's '19th hole' still remains, acting at the social clubhouse. Behind the clubhouse is a floodlit all-weather training pitch.

I walked down to the pitch to find a good vantage point. A new section of covered walkway borders the pitch in front of the changing room building. Behind the goal, to the right, is a further small covered terrace. On the opposite side of the pitch, looking back towards to club buildings is the main grand stand. It is the normal new ground pre-fabricated affair with about 150 seats. Having been extensively developed in the last couple of years Walmer Road obviously has excellent facilities but it is all too squeaky clean with little character, however I am sure this will come with the years.

As I walked round the pitch an announcement was made declaring that the kick off was to be delayed until 8pm. Not what I wanted to hear, especially as it was cold, raining and I was 50 miles from home. I took a seat in the stand in order to shelter from the rain. Unfortunately there is a slight slope to the pitch and the stand is at the bottom so although I was sitting in a tiered stand I felt as if I was still level with the pitch.

Thankfully Kirkley's match-day programme is extremely good so there was plenty to read while I waited for the delayed kick off, apparently caused because the referee had got stuck in traffic. With Kirkley sitting in 4th position in the league with 33 points, the visit of Dereham Town, in 2nd spot with 35 points, promised to be a good contest. Because both clubs were having a good start to the season I was hoping for a good crowd but the abysmal weather must have put a lot of people off.

The game started brightly and the dreadful conditions led me to believe there were bound to be goals. And it was the away team, from Norfolk, who struck first just a few minutes after kick off. One nil to Dereham Town.

Taking up the back row of the stand behind me was a group of teenage lads. They were at the age where it is too uncool to dress appropriately for the conditions. I was wearing my waterproof motorcycle trousers (again), jumper, jacket, hat and gloves. They were wearing bright white trainers and no coats and were complaining how cold they were! Everything was "fucking this...and fucking that". They spoke of their mates from college who were all twats and smirked at the story of one pal who had a video on his mobile phone of him shagging a bird whose name he could not recall. Yes, OK, perhaps I was jealous! I am at that funny mid-30s stage in life. I have realised that I am not going to be a professional footballer or a successful entrepreneur. Thoughts of when to start a family, expiring fixed rate mortgage deals and whether to take out central heating cover occupy my

THE REAL TRACTOR BOYS

mind whilst I still feel like I should be out on the town every Friday night. At times I still only feel 18 yet I was rather disturbed to discover that only Dietmar Hamann in the current Manchester City squad is older than me!

So when one of the likely lads behind me declared that he had a first goal draw ticket timed at 5 minutes I prayed the goal was timed at 6. I know, I was being nasty but their youthful exuberance was making me feel bitter and my heart sank when the announcement declared that Dereham's goal was indeed, scored in the 5th minute. "Fucking get in!" came the cry from behind me. The silver lining was that they buggered off to collect the £20 winnings and spend it in the bar and left the rest of us to actually watch the game.

Dereham were shortly two nil up and Kirkley looked a shambles. The game was not even 20 minutes old and the traffic was one way. The home team made efforts to sure things up and concentrated on not conceding an insurmountable third goal. Rather fortuitously Kirkley were awarded a penalty in the 37th minute. No one appeared to be stepping up to take the spot kick when I noticed the Kirkley goalkeeper was running the full length of the pitch to take the penalty. The keeper, Robert Woodcock, has considerable experience at this level having played for Wroxham and Diss Town. He has the opposite physique to the norm for a goalkeeper being fairly short and stocky. One chap in the stand shouted "God, are we that bad that our keeper is the only guy who can kick a ball?"

Woodcock took the shortest of run ups and let rip at the ball. I do not think I have seen a harder hit penalty. "It almost burst the net" is a commonly used phrase in football but this shot really was that powerful. Many outfield players would have taken off their shirt, run to the corner flag and done a little dance in celebration but Woodcock simply wiped his nose on his sleeve and jogged back to his own goal, attracting high-fives from teammates as he went. No fuss, no nonsense. Upon arrival, he the turned round and bellowed "NOW SORT IT OUT!" He was like some sort of superhero!

With the score at 2-1 to Dereham, I headed to the '19th hole' for half-time refreshments. After nearly knocking over a Christmas tree trying to pour milk into my mug of tea, I embarrassingly made my way outside for the second half. I decided to stand on the opposite side of the pitch near the dugouts, one of my favourite spots at any ground. After about five minutes I realised exactly how cold it really was and how much protection the stand had given me in the first half.

Not only had the referee been delayed getting to the ground but so had Kirkley's top goal scorer Nathen Stone. Having been stuck on a train for 2 hours at Colchester he did not arrive at the ground until half time and he entered the field of play in the 65th minute. With his first touch he set up a goal bringing the scores back level at 2-2.

In a dramatic final few minutes, Kirkley took the lead for the first time, in the 88th minute, only to then concede a penalty in injury time. Unfortunately goalkeeper Woodcock turned out to be human and not a superhero after all, and could not stop Dereham scoring the resulting spot kick to make the score 3-3. What a finish to a very entertaining game.

Ipswich Town had also played on the same night at home against Bristol City. I was a solitary car on the A12 heading back to Ipswich and it was quite startling to see the constant trail of cars laden with Ipswich fans heading out of the town, in the opposite direction. I doubt anyone at Portman Road saw I better game than I had, at a fraction of the cost.

KIRKLEY & PAKEFIELD 3 – 3 DEREHAM TOWN
Attendance 131 @ Walmer Road

CLUB INFO

ADDRESS – Kirkley & Pakefield FC, Walmer Road, LOWESTOFT Suffolk NR33 7L
WEBSITE – www.kirkleyfc.co.uk
ADMISSION - £5.00 + £1.00 programme
MILES TO & FROM CLUB – 87.4 mile

CORNARD UNITED v SWAFFHAM TOWN

RIDGEONS EASTERN COUNTIES LEAGUE DIVISION ONE
Saturday 20th December 2008

Well it was 'take-two' for a visit to watch Cornard United. Unfortunately I was suffering a little, after having my work's Christmas party the night before but felt OK enough to try and find the elusive Blackhouse Lane, this time with Gemma in tow, with the atlas tightly gripped in her hands!

It was an unusually mild December's day and we found the ground with ease this time and it made the troubles I had experienced a couple of weeks ago seem laughable. We parked the car and made our way up the footpath to the ground. A little weirdly, we seemed to be the only people making this short journey, despite kick off being just 10 minutes away. The Saturday before Christmas is traditionally a poor day for football attendances and considering some of the low fan counts Cornard sometimes achieve I was not expecting to have to battle my way through the turnstile, however I did expect to see at least some other people!

We reached the entrance to the ground and were rather surprised to be able to simply walk in. There was a notice that declared the entrance fee as £5 and a small wooden, if somewhat battered, kiosk but no one to take our admittance. The gate is at the corner of the pitch. Carry on straight ahead and you are behind the goal, with a small training pitch to the left. We turned right along a concrete path, with the pitch on the left and trees to the right. At the half way point is a brick built clubhouse with hard standing in front of the pitch. The dugouts are in front of the clubhouse and they really are proper dugouts, with the inhabitant's heads at pitch level. There is a canopy covering part of the hard standing providing onlookers with protection from the rain. The goal end to the right hand side of the pitch is open.

On the opposite side of the pitch to the clubhouse is a pretty decent main stand. Constructed from brick with well tiered steps within, this is one of the most impressive stands in the league. The club state that the stand can accommodate 250 spectators but I reckon it could do a little more. It was therefore a shame that at its peak occupancy in this fixture there were just four people sitting in the stand and two of those were wearing Cornard United tracksuits.

We stood around in front of the clubhouse for a few minutes. Music was being played over the public address system. One other person turned up. The only obvious entrance in to the clubhouse had a sign stating 'Players & Match Officials Only' so we could not see how we were supposed to get in. I was in desperate need of Coca-Cola to assist with my recovery from the night before, and we wanted to pay our admittance and, most importantly, I needed a match day programme. I was seriously worried that there might not be one. How annoying would it be if I failed to get a programme from the penultimate club of my tour!

THE REAL TRACTOR BOYS

Gemma questioned if I had made a mistake with the fixture, as there was not even anyone on the pitch. Usually there are a few of the substitutes warming up and taking pot shots at the goal – but there was no one at 2.55pm!

Then, all of a sudden two teams emerged from the clubhouse led by the match officials and followed by a handful of spectators. Thank goodness - there is a match about to be played. And then one chap passed us with what appeared to be a programme tucked in his coat pocket. The next task then was to find out where he got it from. The good thing was that they were not going to sell out judging by the attendance.

There was an eerie feel to the ground. The lowest attended game I had been to on my tour of Suffolk had been 66 at Debenham LC v Gorsleston but that had been a night game and the lights created an atmosphere. Generally crowds at the smaller clubs are largely populated by mums, dads, friends and girlfriends of the players but there only appeared to be one small group of three family supporters. I counted one away fan. I suppose the fact the both teams kicked off the game in the bottom six of the league did

Blackhouse Lane, home of Cornard United FC

not help but that meant that the game was effectively a six-pointer and almost guaranteed goals.

Cornard United are one of the youngest clubs in the league being founded in 1964. They won promotion to the Eastern Counties League in 1989. The club has won a couple of minor cups in their time and also boast that former professional players Marc Falco, Gary Brooke, Tom English and Peter Coffill have featured in their ranks. The village of Great Cornard is on the edge of the town of Sudbury but because of a sprawling council estate its population is just over 8,000. I guess a large number of non-league fans in the area watch the more successful AFC Sudbury and Cornard United will always have to battle against that.

Just after kick off we were approached by a chap collecting the admission fee. This is the first time I had experienced such a method but I guess it is the most effective way when the crowd is so low. I took the opportunity to enquire about a programme and was shortly in possession of my 19th match day publication and £9 lighter, having paid our admission fees. We were also handed 10 tickets for a Christmas draw for a bottle of whisky. Unless the players were included in the draw I reckoned we had a 1 in 4 chance of winning! Having sorted out the entrance formalities we headed over to the other side of the pitch, mainly because the setting winter sun was in our eyes but also because my wife wanted to watch the female assistant referee running the line, on that side of the pitch.

From our new vantage point we decided to count the attendance ourselves. We figured it was between 16 and 19 depending on whether some of the people around the dugouts were club officials or not. Imagine our surprise when we got home and looked on the league website to see the officially recorded gate was 35. I can honestly say that this cannot be right. I must admit I do not know who qualifies to be included in the gate but I assume that players and officials do not count, just the people who are paying to get in.

The standard of play was not great and it was immediately obvious why both teams were having poor seasons, but Cornard deserved to take their 1-0 lead into the changing rooms at half time. Everyone else followed the players through the 'Players and Match Officials Only' door so we did the same. We found our way

THE REAL TRACTOR BOYS

through to the bar area where a couple of people were watching Sky Sports News for the latest professional scores. With Manchester City playing away at West Bromwich Albion the following day I was more interested in a cup of tea. All of the walls in the clubhouse are adorned with framed replica shirts and pennants representing football clubs from around the World. There were also a couple of press cuttings from when Everton visited the club. In fact, it is stated in the programme that a number of professional clubs have visited Cornard United to prepare for fixtures against Ipswich Town. The ground's record attendance was in 2002 when 400 watched the club play West Ham.

The club house bar's shutters were down – usually a vital source of income for any football club however there was some activity at a small tea bar window however it appeared to be the team's Assistant Manager ferrying cups of tea to the players. He did forget the match officials however as the referee had to come out and request hot beverages for him and his assistants. After they had been catered for I did manage to purchase a cup for myself however my wife does not drink tea or coffee and that is all that was on offer. No soft drinks, chocolate bars or crisps. Another missed opportunity for extra income.

We made our way outside for the second half and it then occurred to us that we reckon it was team manager who collected our admission fees and sold us the programme. We looked around and it did seem that the whole operation was a two-man team. Most non-league football clubs survive because of the support of hard working volunteers. When I got home I did a quick bit of research by looking in my 2003 edition of the 'Non League Club Directory' (I must get a more recent edition!) and realised that the Chris Symes was listed as manager, chairman and secretary. The programme stated that Neil Cottrell was now the chairman but also the Assistant Manager and main sponsor! It also stated that Chris Symes is one of the longest serving managers in the league having held the position for 14 years. He had previously managed Braintree Town and Chelmsford City and been a coach at Arbroath in the Scottish Premiership. I think he also produces the programme and last season was awarded the Groundsman of the Year by the FA. Unbelievable!

These two guys obviously run the club pretty much between them and I am sure they have to dig deep in to their own pockets to make it happen. They must really do it purely for the love and it was therefore quite funny in the second half to see them both texting from the technical area, not really watching the game! Perhaps they were in contact with the one fan in the stand opposite who was offering their opinion on the team's formation.

Cornard quickly scored a second goal, however Swaffham did have a chance to get back in to the game soon afterwards when they were awarded a penalty after a reckless challenge by a Cornard player. Unfortunately for the team from Norfolk, the penalty hit the post. The Cornard Assistant Manager, Chairman and Main Sponsor shouted to the players that they had been let off and should treat the penalty miss as a warning. They obviously took note and took control of the game knocking in another three goals to secure their fifth win in the league.

CORNARD UNITED 5 – 0 SWAFFHAM TOWN *Attendance 35* @ Blackhouse Lane*

* Although we think it was 19 + two teams and their backroom staff!

EXTRA TIME – Due to evening commitments we had to leave the game early (something I hate doing but it was a condition of Gemma's attendance) and therefore we missed the draw for the whisky. Our tickets were numbers 11-20 and I still have them so if we did win please get in touch. Many thanks.

CLUB INFO

ADDRESS – Cornard United FC, Blackhouse Lane, Great Cornard, SUDBURY Suffolk CO10 0NL
WEBSITE– www.clubwebsite.co.uk/cornardunitedfootballclub (not updated since August 2008
ADMISSION - £4.00 + £1.00 programme
MILES TO & FROM CLUB – 44.4 mile

THE REAL TRACTOR BOYS

LOWESTOFT TOWN v KIRKLEY & PAKEFIELD

RIDGEONS EASTERN COUNTIES PREMIER DIVISION
Saturday 27th December 2008

Well this was it! The last game of my 20-club tour of Suffolk. Luckily my busy dash around the county in December had paid off and I was able to end at the Lowestoft derby. Everything had worked out perfectly. We spent Christmas with my family in Northampton and then I had travelled up to Manchester on Boxing Day, to watch Manchester City hammer Hull City 5-1.

THE REAL TRACTOR BOYS

The teams enter at Crown Meadow for the Lowestoft derby

We then drove directly back to Ipswich as my Dad was going to come and stay at ours and then come with me to the Lowestoft game. Unfortunately Dad was suffering with back and ankle problems throughout Boxing Day and by the time we got to Ipswich he was in agony and so he set off home the next morning. Gemma stepped up to the plate and agreed to share my last game with me. I was disappointed Dad could not make it but was still looking forward to more festive football.

Press reports were suggesting a bumper crowd. The Lowestoft derby seems to be growing in stature each season. Crowds of up to 1000 had attended in recent years. Lowestoft Town are by far the most supported non-league football club in Suffolk, and get some of the highest attendances of any club at step 5 level in the whole of the UK. The biggest crowd at Crown Meadow this season, to date, was 842 in an FA Vase game against Harefield United. Kirkley's biggest gate was 210 in a league game against Wroxham.

THE REAL TRACTOR BOYS

I therefore decided to set off at 1pm, leaving us plenty of time to get to the ground, park the car and get through the turnstiles before the 3pm kick off. We were right to give ourselves the early start as when we arrived at the ground a pretty long queue had formed at the entrance. It took us about 10 minutes to pay our admission of £6 each and we could not help but laugh at the contrast with the game we had watched at Cornard United the week before, where we were joined by one man and his dog!

Founded in 1887, the club has played at Crown Meadow since 1890. They were the founding members of the Eastern Counties Football League in 1935 and have unbroken membership since then. Lowestoft Town have won the league title 11 times and have always enjoyed a good following in the town. This was increased last season as the club reached the final of the FA Vase and played at Wembley in front of a crowd of 19,537 (of which 14,000 were Lowestoft fans) against Kirkham & Wesham (now known as AFC Fylde). Lowestoft were ahead for three quarters of the game before conceding two goals in the last ten minutes. The FA Vase adventure plus the fact that the team is top of the league, has meant that the crowds just keep getting bigger and bigger!

I love Crown Meadow. I had visited the ground once before, a couple of years ago, and if it did not take an hour to get to Lowestoft I would have been again before this visit. It is one of only a handful of grounds that has two proper turnstiles (Bury Town, AFC Sudbury and Needham Market are the others that spring to mind). After passing through the gate you find yourself in the corner of the ground with a small club shop to the left adjoining the main brick-built club house. Immediately to the right is a proper area of tiered, covered standing terrace stretching for a third of the pitch. The only down side to this terrace is that it is set too far back from the pitch and the view of the far goal is obscured by the impressive main stand.

I say that the main stand is impressive due to its size and not really its appearance. The stand can seat 466 and is easily the biggest in Suffolk away from Ipswich Town's Portman Road. It is oddly set back from the pitch but the first row of seats are high up, allowing people to pass in front of the stand without blocking the view. It is pretty ugly though, with corrugated asbestos one of the major building materials used. The stand straddles the half way line and every wooden seat was occupied for this fixture

THE REAL TRACTOR BOYS

Beyond the stand is another brick building housing the changing rooms for the players and officials, a snack bar and further toilets for spectators. Behind the far goal is a small, wooden covered area for standing fans which is extremely cosy. Other than that the rest of the ground is open with a concrete path surrounding the pitch. Crown Meadow is one of the few non-league grounds in Suffolk to occupy what I would call a traditional location. What I mean by this is that the ground is found in a residential area, not far from the town centre in the same way as many old league grounds before the trend to build new stadia on the outskirts of towns began. Fans can easily walk to Crown Meadow and the turnstiles are by the side of the street rather than at the end of a long unsurfaced track in the middle of nowhere. And this is what makes Crown Meadow so special and unique amongst the local scene.

There is a large vocal support for 'The Trawlerboys' and the fans sing some great songs about their players and the opposition. Singing fans is a rarity at football grounds of this level and only AFC Sudbury and Ipswich Wanderers can really compete for the singing award...if one existed. It was funny to watch the

The 466 seater main stand at Crown Meadow

Main sponsor **PETROGRAMME** MANAGEMENT SERVICES (U.K.) LTD Match: Reece, Ellie, Aaron & Amber Hope. Ball Sponsor: Mick Chapman (Ridgeons) **515** Five hundred and Fifteen **ADULT**	**Lowestoft Town Football Club** welcomes **Kirkley & Pakefield F.C.** Ridgeons League Premier Division Saturday 27 December 2008 Advance Ticket Sponsor **Foxborough Middle School** School Council
Main sponsor **PETROGRAMME** MANAGEMENT SERVICES (U.K.) LTD Match: Reece, Ellie, Aaron & Amber Hope. Ball Sponsor: Mick Chapman (Ridgeons) **516** Five hundred and Sixteen **ADULT**	**Lowestoft Town Football Club** welcomes **Kirkley & Pakefield F.C.** Ridgeons League Premier Division Saturday 27 December 2008 Advance Ticket Sponsor **Foxborough Middle School** School Council

Match day tickets!

Lowestoft fans singing loud and proud directly outside the changing rooms as the two teams emerged. We originally took up position near one of the goals so I could take some photographs. We then wanted to move to the side of the pitch but due to the large crowd we struggled to get a good position.

We kept thinking how funny it was that there were so many people at this game compared with so few at Cornard the week before. But despite the big crowd something was not quite right and I did not realise what it was when I got home. The attendance was confirmed as a huge 1,523, at least 1,400 more than most of the league games I had been to watch, and almost 1,000 bigger than a normal Lowestoft game. This meant that a large number of people at Crown Meadow for this game were not regular match watchers and were there because of the occasion. As a result a lot of the people seemed more interested in getting chips and talking about Christmas than in the game. The normal game-related banter that I have enjoyed throughout my tour was not there. There were obviously regular fans of both teams present in the crowd however they were being diluted by the masses. I then realised that although the sense of occasion was great at Lowestoft, and I had obviously planned to finish at Crown Meadow with this fixture, I actually enjoyed the experience at Cornard more. It was quirky, odd and funny where as the Lowestoft game was busy with long queues for the loo and difficult to find somewhere to park. I also did not have the freedom to watch the game from whatever angle I wanted.

So what about the game? I had overheard one spectator predict that it would not be a great game technically, and he was correct. The home team looked the stronger and true enough they won the match by two goals to one. But to many spectators it was all about the occasion and what was happening on the field was secondary and so it was to me and in this book.

LOWESTOFT TOWN 2 - 1 KIRKLEY & PAKEFIELD
Attendance 1,523 @ Crown Meadow

CLUB INFO

ADDRESS – Lowestoft Town FC, Crown Meadow, Love Road, LOWESTOFT Suffolk NR32 2PA
WEBSITE – www.lowestofttownfc.co.uk
ADMISSION - £5.00 + £1.20 programme
MILES TO & FROM CLUB – 92.2 miles

FULL TIME

It all started back in April and nine months later I had watched a football match at 20 non-league football grounds in Suffolk. I had not exactly rushed to complete my tour but neither had I dithered. I had also become a season ticket holder at the richest football club in the World! So how does it all fit in?

The simple answer is that I love watching football. In December, on one weekend I watched Manchester City play Everton in front of a crowd of 41,344. The following weekend I watched Cornard United play Swaffham Town in front of 35. I enjoy the glitz and the glamour of the Premier League and watching international footballers wearing the sky blue shirt that means so much to me. The excitement and tension of watching my team is fantastic and extremely addictive.

Watching non-league football is all about the occasion too. I get a real buzz from seeking out a new club and visiting their ground for the first time. The actual act of a football match is raw at non-league level. You can smell the ointments, hear the players swear and feel the tackles. It is a different experience but equally enthralling.

I feel that far too many so-called football fans in this country limit themselves to one team, one league or simply just one sofa. We all know people who have a lot to say about the game yet never venture beyond the four walls of their living room in order to watch a game. Regardless of the amount of action replays, statistics, fan's commentaries, and expert opinions a televised game of football can provide, nothing beats watching a game of live football – in the flesh. Professional football is not cheap to watch. Considering the current financial climate, there has surely never been a better time to take a chance on a local non-league game. With prices starting at £4.00 I guarantee you will not be disappointed!

The Real Tractor Boys *AWARDS*

MY TOP FIVE FOOTBALL GROUNDS IN SUFFOLK

1.   RAM MEADOW – Bury Town. A number of reasons make Ram Meadow my favourite ground. I love the turnstiles in the large wall facing the car park. It has stands with seats on both sides of the pitch and the best covered terraces behind each goal in Suffolk. Ram Meadow can accommodate 1500 fans under cover and the record attendance of 2500 was recorded in an FA Cup fixture against Enfield in the late 1980s. It is therefore very sad that my favourite football ground in Suffolk is set to be no more as the club have announced that they are to move to a new 5000 capacity community stadium at Moreton Hall. The new stadium is set to cost £2million. Ram Meadow is set to be demolished to make way for a new car park.

2.   CROWN MEADOW – Lowestoft Town. Situated in the town centre with turnstiles just off the street, Crown Meadow has an unmistakable charm. Good vocal support and the largest crowds in Suffolk mean that there is always an atmosphere at Crown Meadow. The huge 466 seat main stand is the largest in the county and offers great views of the pitch. Football has been played at Crown Meadow for over 100 years and it could still do with some work to provide better covered standing area but it is still a great ground as it stands.

3.   KING'S MARSH STADIUM – AFC Sudbury. Originally the home of Sudbury Wanderers, the King's Marsh Stadium was chosen to be the home ground when Wanderers merged with Sudbury Town in 1999, to create Amalgamated Football Club Sudbury. Wanderers originally purchased the ground in 1972 and when AFC were formed, the former Town ground was sold for housing and King's Marsh was further developed. The ground features covered terrace behind each goal. A 200 seat stand was erected on the west side of the pitch in 1993 and this was joined by 'The Shed' a tiered, covered terrace on the opposite side of the pitch in 2000. There are extensive plans to further improve the King's Marsh as it still has a number of temporary buildings however the atmosphere is always great and attendances are good.

4.   HUMBER DOUCY LANE – Ipswich Wanderers. I love this ground. Despite recently receiving a lick of paint it still looks pretty rough but it is tightly enclosed, with covered standing on three sides of the ground. It is my favourite place to watch non-league football because you are right alongside the pitch and because the ground is so cramped even a small crowd of 60 or so spectators makes for a great atmosphere. The ground is a collection of rickety wooden buildings and temporary structures and improvements could obviously be made but I love it just as it is.

5.   BLOOMFIELDS – Needham Market. Named after club stalwart, Derrick Bloomfield, Needham Market moved to Bloomfields in 1996 having previously played at Young's Meadow and Crowley Park. The ground has been improved and developed over the last couple of seasons and now features a smart stand and a good area of covered terracing. The new turnstiles are a nice addition and the clubhouse is one of the best in Suffolk. I personally feel that work is needed behind each goal to enclose the ground a little bit more. A unique point is how the players enter the field of play from the top floor of the club house due to the steep hill leading away from the pitch.

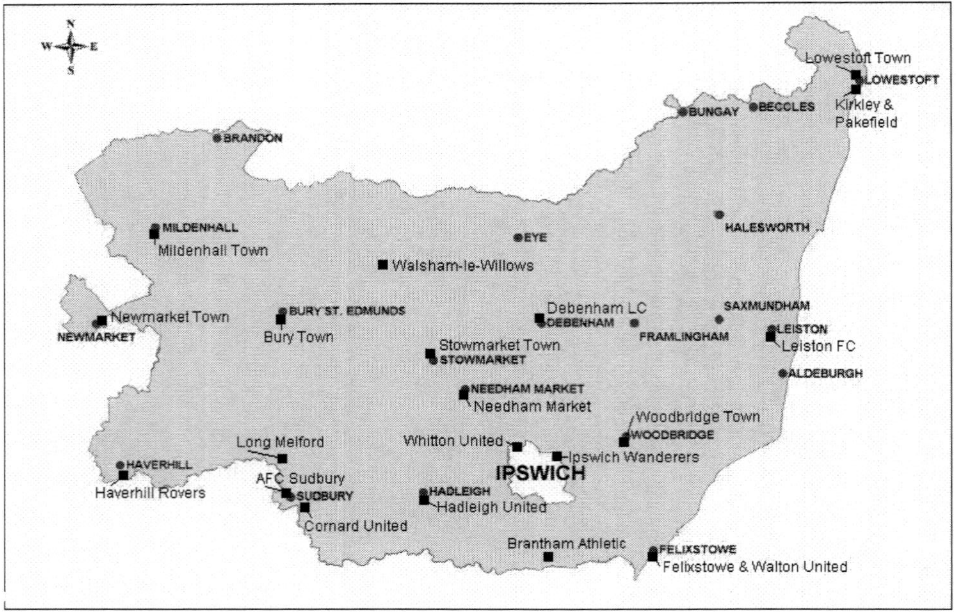
N
W
E
S
Lowestoft Town
LOWESTOFT
Kirkley & Pakefield
BUNGAY
BECCLES
BRANDON
HALESWORTH
MILDENHALL
Mildenhall Town
EYE
Walsham-le-Willows
Newmarket Town
NEWMARKET
BURY ST. EDMUNDS
Bury Town
Debenham LC
DEBENHAM
FRAMLINGHAM
SAXMUNDHAM
LEISTON
Leiston FC
Stowmarket Town
STOWMARKET
ALDEBURGH
NEEDHAM MARKET
Needham Market
Woodbridge Town
WOODBRIDGE
Whitton United
Ipswich Wanderers
IPSWICH
Long Melford
HAVERHILL
Haverhill Rovers
AFC Sudbury
SUDBURY
HADLEIGH
Hadleigh United
Cornard United
Brantham Athletic
FELIXSTOWE
Felixstowe & Walton United

POST MATCH COMMENT

by Graham Smith
(my Dad & fellow Manchester City season ticket holder).

Football, at any level, is about passion, tradition and commitment. It has been one of the most important parts of my life whether playing at non-league level or watching Premiership games.

As a young boy I supported Bolton Wanderers because my Dad and his Dad before him had been avid supporters. Indeed my Grandad used to cycle from Chorlton-cum-Hardy to Burnden Park for both first team and reserve games – a round trip of 60 miles. This passing down teams to future generations is what football is normally all about – not so in my case.

Despite playing for Bolton and being offered professional terms I never felt committed to the club. It was my son's passion for Manchester City that turned me. He was born in Manchester so, for him, there was only ever one team to support. He would write to their various managers (there have been a few in our lifetime), telephone the club call line for news (once amassing a phenomenal phone bill) and go to as many games as he could. His passion and drive were an inspiration to me. I soon became as involved as he was. We are now season ticket holders and our Saturday 'home' games involve 5 hours driving to the game and often longer on the return journey. My Grandad would have been proud of us just as I am so proud of my son.

Our support of Manchester City has been in the words of Kevin Keegan "like a roller-coaster ride" – unfortunately more lows than highs. Every new season has kindled hope that this time we would be up there with the best. Disappointment has followed but there has been no loss of support or commitment. The club has had to live in the shadow of the other Manchester team and it has suffered as a consequence. Now we are the richest club in the World and that makes us the butt of many jokes and jealousy, but this is not our fault. True supporters live through the bad and good times – bring on next season!

THANKS TO:

Firstly, I would like to thank my Wife, Gemma, for tolerating my obsession with football. Without her understanding, this diary would not have been possible, nor would I be able to disappear for 14 hours every other weekend, watching Manchester City.

Secondly, I would like to thank my Dad, Graham, for making my dream of becoming a Manchester City season ticket holder come true.

APOLOGIES:

I would like to apologise if I have caused any upset to anyone in this book. That has not been my intention. I have simply reported my experiences and thoughts and each ground I have visited. Thank you.

ABOUT THE AUTHOR

Matt Smith was born in 1976 in Ashton-Under-Lyne, Greater Manchester. After spending early childhood in Norfolk he grew up in Northampton before moving to Ipswich in 2004, where he now lives with his wife, Gemma.

A varied career has involved selling houses, car insurance, managing a car spares store, driving a bus, followed by 10 years in the civil service and local government.

A Manchester City fan since 1990, Matt enjoys watching football at all levels and looks out for all of the Suffolk clubs. The next challenge is to watch every Suffolk club playing away from home, out of the county!

www.therealtractorboys.co.uk
therealtractorboys@mail.com

Blackline|Press

blurb

blurb.com